# EMPOWERED EATING

---

101 Biohacking Recipes for Quick, Healthy, and Sustainable Weight Loss

Copyright © 2018 Wendi Francis MS, RD, CPC
All Rights Reserved

All content is subject to copyright and may not be reproduced in any form without express written consent of the author.

Although the author and publisher have made every effort to ensure that the information in this book was correct at press time, the author and publisher do not assume and hereby disclaim any liability to any party for any loss, damage, or disruption caused by errors or omissions, whether such errors or omissions result from negligence, accident, or any other cause.

This book is not intended as a substitute for the advice of medical professionals. The reader should regularly consult a medical professional in matters relating to his or her health and particularly with respect to any symptoms that may require diagnosis or medical attention.

Cover Illustration, Book Design and Production by Efluential Publishing, a division of Efluential Marketing, LLC.

www.EfluentialPublishing.com

# Introduction

So, you are getting ready to make a change...FANTASTIC! Our intention in compiling this recipe book is to inspire you to become more creative with your healthful eating. It is amazing how quick, easy, and fun healthy eating can be if you have the right tools. All the recipes in this book create a synergistic, anti-inflammatory, low-glycemic-index lifestyle which will enable your body to look and feel healthier and more youthful.

Authors Wendi Francis MS, RD, CPC, and Dr. Kristen Kells, DC, BSC have been able to help countless people make the changes necessary to enjoy an empowered life. Life is meant to be lived, not to be dull, dreary, painful, or emotionally dead. Life in a healthy body and mind can be enjoyed and celebrated. Imagine a life in which you feel vitality and connection with yourself and others! Imagine a life in which your body does not hurt, ache, or suffer from a disease, a life in which you can feel joy. All of this is attainable!

Don't be a statistic! Currently, the CDC reports that 76 million people in the United States are obese. Furthermore, a review of studies published in the Archives of General Psychiatry found that obese people are at a 55% higher risk of depression, and that obesity contributes to specific diseases like diabetes, heart disease, cancer, and stroke. Many people continue in their poor eating patterns because of bad habits or emotional eating. These recipes can help break those patterns. By eating different foods in different ways, you can transition into a more vibrant, more healthful you. You will not only improve your physical health, but you will also feel better mentally and emotionally.

**Isn't it time to change?**
**Get Empowered and Get Started!**

# Start with the Best Ingredients!

Protein:
- ✓ Organic Chicken
- ✓ Wild-caught Fish
- ✓ Grass-fed Beef
- ✓ Organic Eggs
- ✓ Protein Powder...

This book specifies Pure Vitality Vanilla Protein Powder, which has 10 grams of protein per scoop. If you choose to use a different protein powder, adjust the amount you use to equal the protein serving. In any protein powder, make sure there is no added sugar, caffeine or artificial sweeteners or flavors. Quality counts when it comes to protein powder. We carry professional grade, top quality protein in the clinics and on our E-store.

Vegetables: ✓ Organic

Fruits: ✓ Organic

Healthy Fats:
- ✓ Avocado oil, extra-virgin olive oil, coconut oil, grapeseed oil
- ✓ Oils are generally interchangeable in this book
- ✓ Best oils for high-heat cooking are coconut and grapeseed
- ✓ Organic butter

Spices:

✓ Organic

✓ Best salts: Himalayan sea salt or Celtic sea salt

Condiments and other shelf items:

✓ Plastic can compromise even healthful, organic food. Purchasing in glass jars is best if possible.

✓ Always check ingredients to make sure there is no added sugar or other fillers.

# Finding the Right Balance

In order to make the most of your new eating lifestyle, each recipe includes a table at the bottom which shows servings of protein, vegetables, fruit, and healthy fat.

- ☒ 3 oz. protein
- ☒ 2 servings of vegetables
- ☒ 1 serving of fruit
- ☒ 1-2 servings of healthy fat

The table will serve to help you round out your meal. If everything is checked, like in this sample table, you have a full meal in the one recipe. If you fix a recipe of just meat, you will have to add vegetables and fat to have a full meal.

Note: The shake recipes are meant to serve as "snacks" and only contain one-half serving of protein. If you wish the shake to be used as meal replacement, you will need to add double the protein powder, or add a bit of protein on the side.

Helpful Hints: We want you to experiment, play with recipes, substitute what you like. Just follow your approved food list and make sure portions remain in guidelines. We recommend to save time, cook multiple servings, divide into portions and freeze or refrigerate.

# In Thanks

"First and foremost; thank you to my loving husband, Mark. To my beautiful children; Jana, Lindsey, and Josh. You are true world changers. Huge thank you to my patients! For over 20 years I have been blessed to grow alongside you, guide you, teach you and learn from you. Thank you to so many others that have been a part of this amazing journey. I am incredibly grateful"

— Dr Kristen Kells

---

"I wanted to take this opportunity to thank my amazing husband and children; your tireless and abundant love enables me to do all that I do. A special thank you also to those that helped significantly with this book; Zoe M. DeGeorge, Kristen Cundiff and Karen Chaleki and to all of those that work with me professionally, propelling my expansive thought patterns. Finally, thanks and gratitude to all the patients that I have been honored to work with for the last 25 years. I do not go a day without noticing how enormously blessed I am in my professional life to be able to help so many miraculous people."

— Wendi Francis

# List of Recipes

| | |
|---|---|
| Introduction | 3 |
| In Thanks | 7 |
| List of Recipes | 9-13 |
| About the Authors | 164-165 |

**Shakes**

| | |
|---|---|
| Iced Morning Mocha | 16 |
| Orange Ginger Apple | 17 |
| Watermelon Summer Treat | 18 |
| Mean Green Supreme | 19 |
| Totally Sinful Chocolate Shake | 20 |
| Chocolate Raspberry Delight | 21 |
| Almond Joy | 22 |
| Orange Creamsicle | 23 |
| Vanilla Shake | 24 |
| Very Berry Smoothie | 25 |

**Breakfast**

| | |
|---|---|
| Easy Breakfast Skillet | 28 |
| Veggie Breakfast Bowl | 29 |
| Complete Breakfast Combo | 30 |
| Seaside Breakfast | 31 |
| Baked Egg Cups | 32 |
| Simple Hardboiled Egg and Avocado Bowl | 33 |
| Brussels Sprouts Hash | 34 |
| Spicy Southwestern Breakfast Bowl | 35 |
| Breakfast Salad | 36 |
| Butternut Squash Baked Eggs | 37 |
| Ground Beef Butternut Squash Skillet | 38 |
| Man and Woman's Omelet | 39 |
| Turkey Greens Frittata | 40 |
| Veggie Egg Muffins | 41 |

| | |
|---|---|
| Spaghetti Eggs | 42 |
| Southwest Scramble | 43 |
| Turkey and Butternut Squash Hash | 44 |
| Breakfast Taco Bowl | 45 |
| Cinnamon Chocolate Protein Pancakes | 46 |
| Sweet Vanilla Pancakes | 47 |
| Kaiya's Strawberry Peach Meal | 48 |
| Chris & Karen's Scrumptious Strawberry Waffles | 49 |

## Lunch

| | |
|---|---|
| Easy Salmon Puttanesca | 52 |
| Broccoli Avocado Tuna Bowl | 53 |
| Curried Avocado Egg Salad | 54 |
| Curry Chicken Salad | 55 |
| Orange Marinated Salmon and Vegetable Skewers | 56 |
| Chicken Stuffed Squash | 57 |
| Chicken, Kale and Butternut Squash Soup | 58 |
| Spicy Pepper and Chicken Stir Fry | 59 |
| Baked Mediterranean Chicken | 60 |
| Bruschetta Chicken | 61 |
| Spinach Stuffed Salmon | 62 |
| Chicken, Broccoli and Squash Noodles | 63 |
| Salmon Zucchini Bowl | 64 |
| Turkey and Kale Stew | 65 |
| Slow Cooker Blackberry Chicken | 66 |
| Lemon Almond Chicken Salad | 67 |
| Avocado Salmon Cakes | 68 |

## Appetizers

| | |
|---|---|
| Creamy Lemon Basil Spaghetti Squash | 70 |
| Lime Basil Grilled Zucchini | 71 |
| Stuffed Portobello Mushrooms | 72 |
| Tomato and Eggplant Ragout | 73 |
| Balsamic Chicken Zoodle Soup | 74 |

| | |
|---|---|
| Stuffed Mushrooms | 75 |
| Rosemary Roasted Almonds | 76 |
| Zucchini Chips | 77 |
| Butternut Squash Soup w/Coconut Milk & Cilantro | 78 |
| Spicy Salmon and Cucumber Bites | 79 |
| Red Cabbage Steaks | 80 |
| Balsamic Chicken and Strawberry Skewers | 81 |

**Entrees**

| | |
|---|---|
| Sheet Pan Chicken Dinner | 84 |
| Italian Style Spaghetti Squash Bake | 85 |
| Chicken Fajita Roll-Ups | 86 |
| Balsamic and Herb Chicken | 87 |
| Pan Roasted Blood Orange Chicken | 88 |
| Charmoula Cod | 89 |
| Chicken/Beef Apple Stuffed Acorn Squash | 90 |
| Stuffed Peppers | 91-92 |
| Creamy Butternut Squash Soup | 93 |
| Lime Chicken Kabobs | 94 |
| Korean Steak Kabobs | 95 |
| Zoodles Marinara | 96 |
| Coconut Crusted Cod | 97 |
| Butternut Squash Noodle Hash | 98 |
| Garlic Lover's Salmon | 99 |

**Side Options**

| | |
|---|---|
| "Pasta" Salad | 102 |
| Spanish Cauliflower Rice | 103 |
| Easy Roasted Eggplant | 104 |
| Sautéed Mushroom Berry Chard | 105 |
| Candied Butternut Squash | 106 |
| Grilled Leek and Roasted Bell Pepper Salsa | 107 |
| Dijon and Apple Brussels Sprouts | 108 |
| Zesty Cauliflower Tabbouleh | 109 |

| | |
|---|---|
| Grilled Veggie Platter | 110 |
| Creamy Cauliflower and Leek Soup | 111 |
| BBQ Zucchini | 112 |
| Curry Cauliflower | 113 |
| Balsamic Glazed Meatballs | 114 |
| Caramelized Onion Green Beans w/ Toasted Almond | 115 |
| Herb Baked Butternut Squash | 116 |

## Salads

| | |
|---|---|
| Burger Salad with Mustard Dressing | 118 |
| Strawberry Chicken Spinach Salad with Citrus Dressing | 119 |
| Grilled Veggie & Chicken Salad w/Tomato Vinaigrette | 120-121 |
| Blueberry, Kale and Butternut Squash Salad | 122 |
| Roasted Vegetable Salad with Shallot Vinaigrette | 123 |
| Strawberry Avocado Arugula Salad | 124 |
| Rosemary Grilled Chicken and Peach Salad | 125 |
| Red Cabbage Citrus Salad | 126 |
| Lime Chicken Chopped Salad | 127 |
| Cobb Salad | 128 |
| Steak Cobb Salad with Cilantro Vinaigrette | 129 |
| Spiced Grapefruit and Chicken Watercress Salad | 130 |
| Kale Ginger Detox Salad | 131 |

## Indoor Holiday Celebrations

| | |
|---|---|
| Healthy Roast Turkey | 134 |
| Mashed No-Tatoes | 135 |
| Green Bean "Cauli" Casserole | 136 |
| Cauliflower Pizza | 137-138 |
| Healthful Chili | 139 |
| Delicious Broccoli and Cauliflower Rice | 140 |
| Mock Sweet Potato Casserole | 141 |
| Baked Apple | 142 |
| Cranberry Sauce | 143 |

**Outdoor Holiday Celebrations**

| | |
|---|---|
| Sweet and Crunchy Chicken Slaw | 146 |
| Easy Veggie Salad | 147 |
| Baked Cinnamon Apple Chips | 148 |
| Chicken Wings | 149 |
| Turkey Sliders and Avocado Slaw | 150 |
| Spaghetti and Meatball Bites | 151 |
| Jalapeño Deviled Eggs | 152 |
| Salmon Dip | 153 |
| Low-Carb Cauliflower Hummus | 154 |
| Mock-Tails | 155-156 |

**Desserts**

| | |
|---|---|
| Grilled Peaches | 158 |
| Adam's Apple Sauce | 159 |
| Sweet Blackberry Compote | 160 |
| Charlie's Apple Crumble | 161 |
| Kaiya's Balsamic Peach Compote | 162 |

# Shakes

These shakes are healthful alternatives to a solid meal and can be used in place of a meal, as a snack, or before or after an intense workout. You can also freeze them in a container to take on the go or eat frozen for a delicious dessert alternative.

"A healthy outside starts from the inside."

- Robert Urich

# Iced Morning Mocha

- ✓ 6 oz. decaf coffee
- ✓ ½ scoop unsweetened cocoa powder
- ✓ 1 scoop Pure Vitality Vanilla Protein Powder
- ✓ 1 cup unsweetened almond or coconut milk
- ✓ 10 drops of liquid French Vanilla Stevia
- ✓ 1 cup ice

Put all ingredients into blender.  Blend on high until creamy and frothy.  Serve immediately.

☒ ½ serving of protein  ☐ 1 serving of fruit

☐ 2 servings of vegetables  ☒ 1-2 servings of healthy fat

# Orange Ginger Apple

- ½ green apple
- ½ orange
- 1½ tsp. shredded ginger to taste
- 1 scoop Pure Vitality Vanilla Protein Powder
- 10 drops liquid Vanilla Crème Stevia

---

Put all ingredients into blender. Blend on high until creamy and frothy. Serve immediately.

☒ ½ serving of protein   ☒ 1 serving of fruit

☐ 2 servings of vegetables   ☐ 1-2 servings of healthy fat

# Watermelon Summer Treat

- ✓ 1 cup watermelon
- ✓ 1 scoop Pure Vitality Vanilla Protein Powder
- ✓ 10 drops liquid Vanilla Crème Stevia
- ✓ ½ cup water (optional)

---

Put all ingredients into blender. Blend on high until creamy and frothy. Serve immediately.

☒ ½ serving of protein  ☒ 1 serving of fruit

☐ 2 servings of vegetables  ☐ 1-2 servings of healthy fat

# Mean Green Supreme

- ✓ 1 cup unsweetened coconut milk
- ✓ ½ cup kale
- ✓ 1½ cups cucumber
- ✓ 1 green apple
- ✓ 1 scoop Pure Vitality Vanilla Protein Powder
- ✓ 20 drops liquid Stevia

---

Put all ingredients into blender. Blend on high until creamy and frothy. Serve immediately.

☒ ½ serving of protein ☒ 1 serving of fruit

☒ 2 servings of vegetables ☒ 1-2 servings of healthy fat

# Totally Sinful Chocolate Shake

- ✓ 1 scoop Pure Vitality Vanilla Protein Powder
- ✓ 1 cup unsweetened coconut milk, almond milk, or cashew milk
- ✓ 1-2 Tbsp. cocoa powder
- ✓ 1 cup ice
- ✓ Stevia, to taste

---

Put all ingredients into blender. Blend on high until creamy and frothy. Serve immediately.

☒ ½ serving of protein ☐ 1 serving of fruit

☐ 2 servings of vegetables ☒ 1-2 servings of healthy fat

# Chocolate Raspberry Delight

- ✓ 1 cup unsweetened almond milk
- ✓ 1 scoop Pure Vitality Protein Powder
- ✓ 1 Tbsp. unsweetened cocoa powder
- ✓ 1 cup fresh or frozen raspberries
- ✓ 10 drops liquid Stevia

Put all ingredients into blender. Blend on high until creamy and frothy. Serve immediately.

☒ ½ serving of protein   ☒ 1 serving of fruit

☐ 2 servings of vegetables   ☒ 1-2 servings of healthy fat

# Almond Joy

- ✓ 1 cup unsweetened almond milk
- ✓ 1 tsp. unsalted almond butter
- ✓ 1 tsp. unsweetened shredded coconut
- ✓ 1 Tbsp. cocoa powder
- ✓ 1 scoop Pure Vitality Vanilla Protein Powder
- ✓ 10 drops liquid Stevia

---

Put all ingredients into blender. Blend on high until creamy and frothy. Serve immediately.

☒ ½ serving of protein   ☐ 1 serving of fruit

☐ 2 servings of vegetables   ☒ 1-2 servings of healthy fat

# Orange Creamsicle

- ✓ 1 scoop Pure Vitality Vanilla Protein Powder
- ✓ 1 orange
- ✓ 1 cup unsweetened coconut milk
- ✓ 10 drops liquid Vanilla Crème Stevia
- ✓ ½ cup ice (optional)

---

Put all ingredients into blender. Blend on high until creamy and frothy. Serve immediately.

☒ ½ serving of protein      ☒ 1 serving of fruit

☐ 2 servings of vegetables   ☒ 1-2 servings of healthy fat

# Vanilla Shake

- ✓ 1 scoop Pure Vitality Vanilla Protein Powder
- ✓ 1 cup unsweetened coconut milk, almond milk, or cashew milk
- ✓ 2 tsp. vanilla extract
- ✓ 1 cup ice
- ✓ Stevia, to taste
- ✓ For a delicious holiday treat, add 1 tsp. cinnamon and 1 tsp. nutmeg

---

Put all ingredients into blender.  Blend on high until creamy and frothy.  Serve immediately.

☒ ½ serving of protein     ☐ 1 serving of fruit

☐ 2 servings of vegetables     ☒ 1-2 servings of healthy fat

# Very Berry Smoothie

- ✓ 1 scoop Pure Vitality Vanilla Protein Powder
- ✓ 1 cup unsweetened coconut milk, almond milk, or cashew milk
- ✓ 1 cup frozen strawberries, raspberries, blueberries and/or blackberries
- ✓ 1 cup ice
- ✓ Stevia, to taste (optional)

---

Put all ingredients into blender. Blend on high until creamy and frothy. Serve immediately.

☒ ½ serving of protein    ☒ 1 serving of fruit

☐ 2 servings of vegetables    ☒ 1-2 servings of healthy fat

# Breakfast

Breakfast is an essential part of eating. It really does, "break the fast" that you have gone through all night. It enables the body to begin metabolically burning fuel getting your mind and body ready for the day.

"A winning effort begins with preparation."

Joe Gibbs

# Easy Breakfast Skillet

**Homemade Salsa:**

- ✓ 1 cup tomatoes, diced
- ✓ ¼ cup onion, diced
- ✓ Cilantro to taste
- ✓ 1 clove garlic, minced
- ✓ 1 Tbsp. lime juice
- ✓ 1 jalapeño pepper, minced
- ✓ Salt and pepper to taste

- ✓ 3 oz. ground turkey or beef
- ✓ 1 tsp. butter
- ✓ 2 cups homemade salsa (see left column)
- ✓ 1 egg
- ✓ ⅛ avocado (optional)

---

1. Combine all salsa ingredients in a bowl up to 8 hours ahead.
2. Melt butter in a skillet and add meat until browned.
3. Mix in salsa and let cook together for 2-3 minutes.
4. Add egg and cover skillet for 7 minutes or until the egg white is opaque.

☒ 3 oz of protein  ☐ 1 serving of fruit

☒ 2 servings of vegetables  ☒ 1-2 servings of healthy fat

# Veggie Breakfast Bowl

**Homemade Salsa:**
- ✓ 1 tsp. coconut oil
- ✓ 1 cup asparagus, bite-sized pieces
- ✓ ½ cup kale leaves, shredded
- ✓ 1 batch lemon dressing
- ✓ ½ cup raw Brussels sprouts, shredded
- ✓ 2 eggs cooked any way
- ✓ 6 sliced almonds
- ✓ Crushed red pepper to taste

**Lemon Dressing**
- ✓ 1 tsp. olive oil
- ✓ 2 Tbsp. lemon juice
- ✓ 2 tsp. Dijon mustard
- ✓ 1 clove garlic, minced
- ✓ Salt and pepper to taste

---

1. In a small bowl, whisk lemon dressing ingredients up to 8 hours ahead.
2. Heat oil in a large sauté pan over medium-high heat. Add asparagus and sauté for 4-5 minutes, stirring occasionally, until tender. Remove from heat and set aside.
3. Meanwhile, in a large mixing bowl, combine the kale and lemon dressing. Use your fingers to massage the dressing into the kale until the leaves are dark and softened. Add Brussels sprouts and asparagus and toss until combined.
4. In a bowl, layer kale salad, 2 eggs, almonds, and crushed red pepper.

☒ 3 oz of protein  ☐ 1 serving of fruit

☒ 2 servings of vegetables  ☒ 1-2 servings of healthy fat

# Complete Breakfast Combo

- ¾ cup butternut squash, cubed
- ¼ cup red onion, chopped
- 1 tsp. melted coconut oil
- ½ tsp. cinnamon
- Sprinkle of salt
- 1 cup spring mix or baby spinach
- 1 Granny Smith apple, thinly sliced
- 2 eggs cooked any way
- 1 tsp. olive oil
- 2 tsp. apple cider vinegar

---

1. Preheat oven to 450°.
2. In a bowl, mix butternut squash, red onion, melted coconut oil, cinnamon, and salt. Turn onto a baking sheet and roast for 30 minutes or until squash is cooked through. Remove and let cool.
3. Layer a salad bowl with greens, squash mixture, apple slices, and cooked eggs. Drizzle with olive oil and vinegar.

☒ 3 oz of protein ☒ 1 serving of fruit

☒ 2 servings of vegetables ☒ 1-2 servings of healthy fat

# Seaside Breakfast

- ✓ 2 oz. canned tuna in water, drained
- ✓ 1 egg
- ✓ 1 cup marinated artichoke hearts, chopped (marinated in water not oil)
- ✓ 1 cup arugula
- ✓ Salt and pepper to taste

---

1. Preheat oven to 375°.
2. Place tuna in a small bowl and use a fork to break apart the meat. Add artichoke hearts and toss to combine.
3. Place tuna and artichoke mixture into a small oven-safe dish. Break egg on top of the tuna mixture, and salt and pepper to taste.
4. Bake for about 10-12 minutes, or until eggs are cooked to preference.
5. Serve over arugula.

☒ 3 oz of protein ☐ 1 serving of fruit

☒ 1-2 servings of vegetables ☐ 1-2 servings of healthy fat

# Baked Egg Cups

- ✓ 12 eggs
- ✓ ½ tsp. salt
- ✓ ½ tsp. black pepper
- ✓ 1 tsp. coconut oil
- ✓ ½ cup orange bell pepper, chopped
- ✓ ½ cup onion, chopped
- ✓ ½ cup broccoli, chopped into small pieces
- ✓ ½ cup mushrooms, sliced
- ✓ 2 Tbsp. fresh parsley
- ✓ 1 tsp. coconut oil or cooking spray

1. Preheat oven to 375°.
2. Grease twelve-cup muffin tin or line with silicone baking cups.
3. Place eggs into a large bowl and whisk to combine. Season with salt and pepper.
4. Heat oil in a skillet over medium heat. Add chopped veggies and mushrooms and sauté for about 5-6 minutes, until they soften slightly.
5. Add sautéed veggies into the bowl with the whisked eggs. Add parsley and mix well.
6. Pour mixture into muffin cups.
7. Bake for 17-20 minutes, or until the egg cups are no longer jiggly and an inserted toothpick comes out clean.
8. Makes 6 servings. 1 serving = 2 muffin cups

☒ 3 oz of protein          ☐ 1 serving of fruit

☒ 2 servings of vegetables  ☒ 1-2 servings of healthy fat

# Simple Hardboiled Egg and Avocado Bowl

- ✓ 2 hard boiled eggs, chopped
- ✓ ⅛ large avocado, chopped
- ✓ 1 Tbsp. red onion, finely chopped
- ✓ 1 Tbsp. red bell pepper, finely chopped
- ✓ Salt and pepper to taste

---

Combine eggs, avocado, onion, and bell pepper in a bowl. Salt and pepper to taste.

☒ 3 oz of protein  ☐ 1 serving of fruit

☐ 2 servings of vegetables  ☒ 1-2 servings of healthy fat

# Brussels Sprouts Hash

- ✓ 1 cup butternut squash, cubed
- ✓ ½ cup red onion, finely diced
- ✓ 1 clove garlic, minced
- ✓ ½ cup Brussels sprouts, sliced
- ✓ 1 tsp. olive oil or coconut oil
- ✓ Salt and pepper to taste
- ✓ 2 eggs

---

1. Heat a sauté pan over medium heat. Add the butternut squash, onion, and garlic and cook for 5-7 minutes, stirring occasionally, until soft.
2. Stir in the Brussels sprouts and oil.
3. Season generously with salt and pepper.
4. Sauté for 8-10 minutes until the Brussels sprouts are bright green and fork tender.
5. Make two small wells in the hash and crack an egg into each. Cover and cook until the eggs are set.

☒ 3 oz of protein  ☐ 1 serving of fruit

☒ 2 servings of vegetables  ☒ 1-2 servings of healthy fat

# Spicy Southwestern Breakfast Bowl

- ✓ ⅔ cup butternut squash, cubed
- ✓ 2 tsp. olive oil, divided
- ✓ Salt and pepper to taste
- ✓ 1 tsp. chili powder
- ✓ ⅓ cup onion, diced
- ✓ ¼ cup green bell pepper, diced
- ✓ ¼ cup red bell pepper, diced
- ✓ 1 small jalapeño, diced
- ✓ ½ cup fresh spinach
- ✓ 2 eggs
- ✓ ⅛ avocado, diced (optional)

---

1. Preheat oven to 375°.
2. Place the butternut squash on a rimmed baking sheet and drizzle with 1 tsp. oil. Sprinkle with salt, pepper, and chili powder. Bake until tender, turning once.
3. Meanwhile, heat 1 tsp. oil in a skillet over medium-high heat. Add onion, bell pepper, and jalapeño and sauté for 5-6 minutes until soft.
4. Add spinach and cook until wilted.
5. In a separate skillet, cook eggs to desired preference, seasoning with salt and pepper.
6. In a bowl, layer butternut squash, veggie mixture, eggs, and avocado.

☒ 3 oz of protein ☐ 1 serving of fruit

☒ 2 servings of vegetables ☒ 1-2 servings of healthy fat

# Breakfast Salad

**Dressing:**
- ✓ 1 Tbsp. fresh dill, chopped
- ✓ 2 Tbsp. lemon juice
- ✓ 1 Tbsp. apple cider vinegar
- ✓ 1 tsp. olive oil

**Salad:**
- ✓ ¼ cup asparagus, bite-sized pieces
- ✓ ¼ cup butternut squash, cubed
- ✓ Salt and pepper to taste
- ✓ 1 cup chopped kale; stems removed
- ✓ ½ cup spring mix
- ✓ 2 fried or boiled egg
- ✓ 1 tsp. olive oil

---

1. Preheat oven to 425°. Line a baking sheet with parchment paper.
2. Combine all dressing ingredients in a jar. Seal and shake vigorously until dressing are combined. Set aside.
3. Put asparagus and squash on baking sheet and drizzle with oil, salt, and pepper and roast for about 15 minutes until tender.
4. In a bowl, toss kale, spring mix, asparagus, and butternut squash.
5. Add eggs to the top and serve.

☒ 3 oz of protein    ☐ 1 serving of fruit

☒ 2 servings of vegetables    ☒ 1-2 servings of healthy fat

# Butternut Squash Baked Eggs

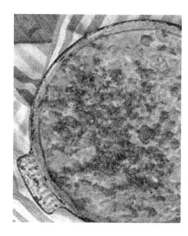

- ✓ 1 cup butternut squash, cubed
- ✓ 2 eggs
- ✓ ¼ cup unsweetened almond milk
- ✓ 1 clove garlic, minced
- ✓ 2 tsp. olive oil, divided
- ✓ 1 cup leeks, white and light green parts only, sliced
- ✓ 2 Tbsp. chopped fresh herbs (mix of sage and thyme)
- ✓ ½ tsp. balsamic vinegar
- ✓ Salt and pepper to taste

---

1. Preheat oven to 400° and line a baking sheet with parchment paper.
2. Place squash on baking sheet and drizzle with 1 tsp. oil. Salt and pepper to taste. Roast until squash is tender, about 20 minutes.
3. In a small bowl, whisk together eggs, almond milk, and garlic. Set aside.
4. Heat 1 tsp. olive oil in an oven-safe skillet over medium heat. Add leeks and a pinch of salt and pepper and sauté until soft, about 1 minute. Stir in herbs and squash and sauté for another minute.
5. Add balsamic vinegar and stir so that nothing is sticking to the bottom of the pan.
6. Add the egg mixture and spread in an even layer. Transfer the skillet to the oven and bake for 20 to 25 minutes, or until the eggs are set and the edges are golden brown.

☒ 3 oz of protein ☐ 1 serving of fruit

☒ 2 servings of vegetables ☒ 1-2 servings of healthy fat

# Ground Beef Butternut Squash Skillet

- ✓ 1 cup butternut squash, cooked
- ✓ ½ cup spinach, chopped
- ✓ 1 tsp. coconut oil
- ✓ ¼ cup onion, chopped
- ✓ ¼ cup celery stalks, chopped
- ✓ 2 cloves garlic, minced
- ✓ ½ tsp. salt
- ✓ 2 oz. ground beef
- ✓ ¼ tsp. white pepper
- ✓ 1 tsp. cumin
- ✓ 1 tsp. garam masala
- ✓ ½ tsp. coriander
- ✓ 1 egg
- ✓ ⅛ avocado, sliced

1. Preheat oven to 375°.
2. Cook spinach in the microwave for one minute or until wilted. Allow to cool and squeeze out as much liquid as you can.
3. While the spinach is cooling, scoop the flesh out of the cooked squash and set aside.
4. Heat oil in a skillet over medium-high heat and add onion, celery, garlic, and salt. Sauté about 2-3 minutes, until slightly softened.
5. Add ground beef, white pepper, cumin, coriander, and garam masala and cook until the beef is browned.
6. Add squash and spinach and mix lightly.
7. Create a well in the mixture and crack an egg into it. Sprinkle with salt and pepper.
8. Bake for 12-15 minutes, or until egg is set.
9. Garnish with avocado and serve immediately.

☒ 3 oz of protein  ☐ 1 serving of fruit

☒ 2 servings of vegetables  ☒ 1-2 servings of healthy fat

# Man and Woman's Omelette

- ✓ 2 eggs
- ✓ 1 cup fresh spinach
- ✓ ¼ cup cremini mushrooms, sliced
- ✓ ¼ cup green onions, sliced fine
- ✓ 4 shakes black pepper
- ✓ 1 tsp. garlic powder
- ✓ 2 tsp. coconut oil, divided
- ✓ ½ cup salsa

---

1. Heat 1 tsp. oil in a skillet over medium heat. Add spinach, mushrooms, and onions and sauté until softened. Add about half of the seasonings to the vegetables. When done, transfer the cooked veggie mix to a plate.
2. In the same pan, and using the other tsp. oil, scramble the eggs, add the other half of the seasonings, and form into a flat pancake.
3. Transfer the veggies back onto the eggs and fold the eggs over to create your omelette.
4. Serve with salsa.

☒ 3 oz of protein     ☐ 1 serving of fruit

☒ 2 servings of vegetables     ☒ 1-2 servings of healthy fat

# Turkey Greens Frittata

- ✓ 2 oz. cooked, shredded turkey
- ✓ 1½ cups finely chopped greens (collards, kale, or spinach)
- ✓ 4 cloves garlic, minced
- ✓ ¼ cup onion, chopped
- ✓ 1 egg
- ✓ 2 tsp coconut oil
- ✓ ¼ cup tomato, sliced

---

1. Preheat oven to 350°. Stir everything (except the tomato) together until well combined.
2. Pour into a small casserole dish, top with the tomato slices, and bake until the egg is fully set.

☒ 3 oz of protein  ☐ 1 serving of fruit

☒ 2 servings of vegetables  ☒ 1-2 servings of healthy fat

# Veggie Egg Muffins

- 1 tsp. olive oil
- ⅓ cup onion, chopped
- 1 clove garlic, minced
- ⅓ cup zucchini, shredded
- ⅓ cup red bell pepper, chopped
- 2 eggs
- 1 cup arugula, roughly chopped
- Salt and pepper to taste

---

1. Preheat oven to 375°. Grease a muffin tin with oil or spray and set aside.
2. Heat oil in a large skillet over medium heat. Add onion and garlic and sauté for about 4 minutes.
3. Add in zucchini and red bell pepper, cooking an additional 2 minutes. Fill each muffin cup about ⅔ full of veggie mixture.
4. In a large bowl, whisk together eggs, arugula, salt, and pepper and fill each muffin cup evenly, being careful not to overfill.
5. Bake muffins for about 20 minutes, until risen and slightly browned.

☒ 3 oz of protein  ☐ 1 serving of fruit

☒ 2 servings of vegetables  ☒ 1-2 servings of healthy fat

# Spaghetti Eggs

- ✓ 2 eggs
- ✓ 1 cup spaghetti sauce (no sugar)
- ✓ 1 cup vegetable of choice

---

1. Scramble eggs as usual.
2. Stir in spaghetti sauce until heated through. Add vegetable to the sauce or simply eat on the side.

☒ 3 oz of protein   ☐ 1 serving of fruit

☒ 2 servings of vegetables   ☒ 1-2 servings of healthy fat

# Southwest Scramble

- ✓ 2 eggs
- ✓ ¼ tsp. cumin
- ✓ ½ tsp. oregano
- ✓ ¼ tsp. paprika
- ✓ Salt and pepper to taste
- ✓ 1 tsp. coconut oil
- ✓ ¼ cup orange bell pepper, chopped
- ✓ ¼ cup red bell pepper, chopped
- ✓ ¼ cup zucchini, grated
- ✓ ¼ cup cherry tomatoes, halved
- ✓ 1 cup green onion, chopped
- ✓ ¼ cup cilantro, chopped
- ✓ ⅛ avocado

---

1. In a medium bowl, whisk together eggs, cumin, oregano, paprika, salt, and pepper until egg mixture is foamy. Set aside.
2. Heat oil in a large skillet over medium-high heat. Add bell peppers and sauté until soft and fragrant, about 4 minutes. Add zucchini, tomatoes, and green onions and continue cooking another minute.
3. Add in egg mixture and stir until eggs are cooked, about 3-5 minutes. Mix in cilantro.
4. Top with avocado slices.

☒ 3 oz of protein     ☐ 1 serving of fruit

☒ 2 servings of vegetables     ☒ 1-2 servings of healthy fat

# Turkey and Butternut Squash Hash

- ✓ 1 cup butternut squash, cubed
- ✓ 1 tsp. coconut oil
- ✓ ⅓ cup onion, chopped
- ✓ 1 clove garlic, minced
- ✓ 3 oz. ground turkey
- ✓ ⅓ cup zucchini, diced
- ✓ ⅓ cup red bell pepper, diced
- ✓ 1 tsp. ground cumin
- ✓ 1 tsp. smoked paprika
- ✓ ½ tsp. chili powder
- ✓ ½ tsp. salt
- ✓ 1 tsp. fresh parsley, finely chopped

1. Bring a medium pot of water to a boil and add squash and simmer until softened. Drain in a colander and set aside.
2. Heat oil in a large nonstick skillet over medium heat and sauté onion and garlic about 3 minutes. Add ground turkey and cook until browned.
3. Add squash, zucchini, bell pepper, cumin, paprika, chili powder, and salt, mixing well, and cook until vegetables are slightly caramelized and crispy, about 5 minutes.
4. Remove from heat and top with fresh parsley.

☒ 3 oz of protein  
☐ 1 serving of fruit  
☒ 2 servings of vegetables  
☒ 1-2 servings of healthy fat

# Breakfast Taco Bowl

**Taco Meat:**
- ✓ 2 oz. ground beef
- ✓ 2 Tbsp. chili powder
- ✓ 1 tsp. oregano
- ✓ 1 tsp. cumin
- ✓ ½ tsp. smoked paprika
- ✓ 1 tsp. black pepper
- ✓ 1 tsp. salt
- ✓ ¾ cup water

**Salad Ingredients:**
- ✓ 1½ cups lettuce, chopped
- ✓ ½ cup bell pepper, chopped
- ✓ ⅛ avocado, smashed
- ✓ 1 egg

---

1. Heat a skillet over medium-high heat. Add ground beef and brown, draining fat, as necessary.
2. Add all spices and water. Let the meat simmer for approximately 10 minutes or until much of the liquid is gone.
3. Meanwhile, fry the egg in a separate pan and set aside.
4. Layer a bowl with lettuce, taco meat, and fried egg.

☒ 3 oz of protein　　　☐ 1 serving of fruit

☒ 2 servings of vegetables　　　☒ 1-2 servings of healthy fat

# Cinnamon Chocolate Protein Pancakes

- ✓ 2 scoops Pure Vitality Vanilla Protein Powder
- ✓ 1 scoop unsweetened cocoa powder
- ✓ 1 egg
- ✓ 2 Tbsp. unsweetened almond milk
- ✓ 1 tsp. baking powder
- ✓ 1 tsp. cinnamon
- ✓ 1 tsp. coconut oil
- ✓ 1 cup fresh or frozen berries

1. Mix the protein powder, cocoa powder, almond milk, cinnamon, baking powder, and eggs in a bowl.
2. Heat oil on a griddle over medium heat and add pancake batter. Cook about 2 minutes on each side.
3. Top with fresh berries or heat frozen berries on stovetop with 3 drops Stevia to make a fruit sauce. (See Sweet Blackberry Compote on p. 160 or Kaiya's Balsamic Peach Compote on p. 163.)

☒ 3 oz of protein  ☒ 1 serving of fruit

☐ 2 servings of vegetables  ☒ 1-2 servings of healthy fat

# Sweet Vanilla Pancakes

- ✓ 2 scoops Pure Vitality Vanilla Protein Powder
- ✓ 1 tsp. vanilla extract
- ✓ 1 egg
- ✓ 2 Tbsp. unsweetened almond milk
- ✓ 1 tsp. baking powder
- ✓ Cinnamon, to taste
- ✓ 1 tsp. coconut oil
- ✓ 1 cup fresh or frozen berries

1. Mix protein powder, vanilla extract, egg, almond milk, baking powder, and cinnamon in a bowl.
2. Heat oil on a griddle over medium heat and add pancake batter. Cook about 2 minutes on each side.
3. Top with fresh berries or heat frozen berries on stovetop with 3 drops Stevia to make a fruit sauce. (See Sweet Blackberry Compote on p. 160 or Kaiya's Balsamic Peach Compote on p. 163.)

☒ 3 oz of protein        ☒ 1 serving of fruit

☐ 2 servings of vegetables    ☒ 1-2 servings of healthy fat

# Kaiya's Strawberry Peach Meal

**Crust:**
- ✓ 1 cup slivered almonds
- ✓ 1 Tbsp. melted coconut oil
- ✓ 1 tsp. cinnamon

**Filling:**
- ✓ 2 cups peaches, frozen
- ✓ 2 cups strawberries, frozen
- ✓ 2 tsp. vanilla extract
- ✓ 1 tsp. cinnamon
- ✓ 15 drops liquid Stevia

1. Preheat oven to 375°.
2. Crush slivered almonds in a zip lock bag.
3. Add oil into bag and mix thoroughly.
4. Transfer to a pie pan and sprinkle with cinnamon.
5. In a bowl, mix peaches and strawberries with vanilla extract, cinnamon, and Stevia.
6. Add mixture on top of almond crust.
7. Bake for 45 minutes.
8. Makes 4 servings

☒ 3 oz of protein ☒ 1 serving of fruit

☐ 2 servings of vegetables ☒ 1-2 servings of healthy fat

# Chris and Karen's Scrumptious Strawberry Waffles

- ✓ 1 cup almond flour/meal
- ✓ ¼ tsp. baking powder
- ✓ ⅛ tsp. salt
- ✓ ⅛ tsp. cinnamon
- ✓ ⅛ tsp. nutmeg
- ✓ ⅓ cup unsweetened applesauce
- ✓ 2 eggs, beaten
- ✓ 2 cups strawberries, sliced
- ✓ Coconut oil

1. Preheat waffle maker to medium heat.
2. In a medium bowl, whisk together almond flour, baking powder, salt, cinnamon, and nutmeg.
3. Add applesauce, eggs, and water to the dry mixture. Whisk to combine.
4. Lightly coat waffle maker with oil.
5. Pour waffle batter in and wait until waffle maker indicates "Done."
6. Remove waffle with fork and repeat steps 4 and 5 until all the batter is used.
7. Top with strawberries.
8. Makes four 8" waffles. 1 serving = 2 waffles

☒ 3 oz of protein     ☒ 1 serving of fruit

☐ 2 servings of vegetables     ☒ 1-2 servings of healthy fat

# Lunch

Throughout the day your food provides energy and nourishment to your working body.

Feeding it a healthful lunch helps you maintain your energy levels, allowing you to complete all your tasks with zeal.

"Take care of your body. It's the only place you have to live."

Jim Rohn

# Easy Salmon Puttanesca

**For the Salmon:**
- ✓ 3 oz. salmon
- ✓ ½ tsp. garlic powder
- ✓ ½ tsp. salt
- ✓ ½ tsp. black pepper

**Puttanesca Sauce:**
- ✓ 2 cloves garlic, minced
- ✓ ½ cup sun-dried tomatoes
- ✓ ½ cup Roma tomatoes, chopped
- ✓ 1 tsp. olive oil
- ✓ ⅓ cup onion, chopped
- ✓ 1 tsp. lemon juice
- ✓ 1 tsp. parsley
- ✓ 1 tsp. oregano
- ✓ ½ tsp. basil
- ✓ ½ tsp. crushed red pepper
- ✓ 6 Kalamata olives
- ✓ 1 cup zucchini, diced

---

1. Preheat oven to 350°. Line a baking sheet with parchment paper and set aside.
2. In a food processor or high-speed blender, combine all the puttanesca sauce ingredients and pulse for 1-2 minutes. You don't want it fully smooth, so don't overmix.
3. Transfer mixture to a medium saucepan and simmer over low heat for 10 minutes.
4. Put salmon on baking sheet and sprinkle with spices. Put in oven and bake all the way through, 5-10 minutes.
5. Ladle the puttanesca sauce on a plate and top with the salmon.

☒ 3 oz of protein   ☐ 1 serving of fruit

☒ 2 servings of vegetables   ☒ 1-2 servings of healthy fat

# Broccoli Avocado Tuna Bowl

- ✓ 1 tsp. coconut oil
- ✓ ¼ cup red onion, chopped
- ✓ 1 cup broccoli florets
- ✓ 3 oz. canned tuna in water, drained
- ✓ ⅛ avocado
- ✓ 2 tsp. Braggs Liquid Amino
- ✓ 1 Tbsp. roasted sunflower seeds
- ✓ ¾ cup cauliflower rice

---

1. Heat oil in a small skillet over medium heat. Add onion and sauté 3-4 minutes.
2. Add broccoli florets and sauté until their color has brightened. Add tuna, avocado, and Braggs Liquid Amino to the skillet. Toss to combine and mash the avocado into the mixture a bit.
3. Cook over medium-low heat until everything is warmed through.
4. Serve over cauliflower rice and top with sunflower seeds.

☒ 3 oz of protein  ☐ 1 serving of fruit

☒ 2 servings of vegetables  ☒ 1-2 servings of healthy fat

# Curried Avocado Egg Salad

- ✓ 2 hard-boiled eggs, chopped
- ✓ ⅛ avocado, cubed
- ✓ ½ Tbsp. Dijon mustard
- ✓ 1-2 tsp. cucumbers, chopped (optional)
- ✓ 1-2 tsp. green onion, chopped
- ✓ 1 tsp. apple cider vinegar
- ✓ ¾ tsp. curry powder
- ✓ Salt and pepper to taste

---

1. Add all ingredients to a bowl and mix thoroughly.

☒ 3 oz of protein  ☐ 1 serving of fruit

☐ 2 servings of vegetables  ☒ 1-2 servings of healthy fat

# Curry Chicken Salad

- ✓ 2 oz. cooked, shredded chicken
- ✓ 6 almonds, chopped
- ✓ 3 Tbsp. fresh chives, chopped
- ✓ 3½ tsp. curry powder
- ✓ 1 tsp. salt
- ✓ 1 Tbsp. Vegenaise
- ✓ 1 cup blueberries

---

1. Add shredded chicken, almonds, chives, curry powder, and salt to a large bowl and mix.
2. Add Vegenaise and mix until combined, and then gently fold in the blueberries.

☒ 3 oz of protein  ☒ 1 serving of fruit

☐ 2 servings of vegetables  ☐ 1-2 servings of healthy fat

# Orange Marinated Salmon and Vegetable Skewers

- ✓ 3 oz. salmon
- ✓ Juice of 1 orange
- ✓ Salt to taste
- ✓ 1 tsp. olive oil
- ✓ 1 clove garlic, crushed
- ✓ ¼ cup red bell pepper, bite-sized pieces
- ✓ ½ cup eggplant, bite-sized pieces
- ✓ ½ cup zucchini, bite-sized pieces
- ✓ ¼ cup red onion, bite-sized pieces
- ✓ ½ cup cherry tomatoes
- ✓ 1 cup pineapple, bite-sized pieces

---

1. To make the marinade, combine juice of 1 orange, salt, oil, and garlic in a bowl.
2. Remove skin and bones from salmon. Cut into bite-sized pieces and marinate, ideally for a few hours.
3. Meanwhile, cut veggies and pineapple into bite-sized pieces. Do not cut the cherry tomatoes.
4. Thread the salmon, veggies, and pineapple onto the skewers.
5. Preheat grill on medium to high heat and grease with olive oil. Grill salmon skewers for about 10 minutes.

☒ 3 oz of protein  ☒ 1 serving of fruit

☒ 2 servings of vegetables  ☒ 1-2 servings of healthy fat

# Chicken Stuffed Squash

- ✓ 3" wide, 3" deep acorn squash, seeded and halved
- ✓ 2 tsp. olive oil
- ✓ ½ tsp. salt

**Filling:**
- ✓ 3 oz. cooked, shredded chicken
- ✓ 1 cup red onion, chopped
- ✓ 1 Tbsp. fresh rosemary, chopped
- ✓ 1 tsp. oregano
- ✓ 1 tsp. garlic powder
- ✓ ½ tsp. salt
- ✓ ½ cup broth/stock

1. Preheat oven to 400° and line a baking sheet with parchment paper.
2. After halving and seeding, brush squash with olive oil and sprinkle with salt.
3. Place squash open side down and bake for 25-30 minutes or until squash is tender.
4. Meanwhile, add all the filling ingredients to a large bowl and mix until combined.
5. Divide the filling into each acorn squash and then bake for another 15-20 minutes or until filling is hot.

- ☒ 3 oz of protein
- ☒ 2 servings of vegetables
- ☐ 1 serving of fruit
- ☒ 1-2 servings of healthy fat

# Chicken, Kale and Butternut Squash Soup

- ✓ 1 Tbsp. butter
- ✓ 4 cups butternut squash, chopped
- ✓ 1 bell pepper, chopped
- ✓ 1 Tbsp. garlic, minced
- ✓ 4 cups kale, ribs removed and chopped
- ✓ 2 Tbsp. fresh thyme, chopped
- ✓ ½ cup fresh basil, chopped
- ✓ 4 cups cooked, shredded chicken
- ✓ 6 cups bone broth or stock
- ✓ 1 tsp. salt
- ✓ 1 tsp. black pepper

1. Heat butter in a large soup pot over medium-high heat. Add squash and bell pepper and sauté for about 5 minutes.
2. Add the garlic, kale, thyme, and basil and mix thoroughly.
3. Add chicken, broth, salt, and pepper and simmer for 20-25 minutes or until squash is soft.
4. Makes approximately 4 servings. 1 serving = 1 cup

☒ 3 oz of protein  ☐ 1 serving of fruit

☒ 2 servings of vegetables  ☒ 1-2 servings of healthy fat

# Spicy Pepper and Chicken Stir Fry

- 3 oz. chicken breast, cut into 1" slices
- 1 tsp. coconut oil
- 1 tsp. cumin seeds
- 2 cups green, red, and orange bell pepper, thinly sliced
- 1 tsp. garam masala
- 2 tsp. black pepper
- Salt to taste
- Scallions (optional)

**For the marinade:**

- 1 clove garlic, minced
- 1 tsp. ginger, minced
- 1 Tbsp. black pepper
- 2 tsp. salt
- ¼ tsp. turmeric

---

1. Place all the marinade ingredients into a Ziploc bag. Add the chicken, close the bag, and shake to coat. Marinate in the refrigerator for at least 30 minutes, or up to 6 hours.
2. Heat oil in a wok or large sauté pan over medium-high heat. Add cumin seeds and sauté for 2-3 minutes.
3. Add the marinated chicken and let sauté for 5 minutes. Stir the chicken until it begins to brown, then add the peppers, garam masala, and black pepper. Sprinkle with salt.
4. Cook for 4-5 minutes, stirring regularly, or until the bell pepper is cooked to desired doneness. Top with scallions.

☒ 3 oz of protein  ☐ 1 serving of fruit

☒ 2 servings of vegetables  ☒ 1-2 servings of healthy fat

# Baked Mediterranean Chicken

- 3 oz. chicken breast
- 2 sprigs fresh rosemary
- ¼ cup sun-dried tomatoes
- 1½ cup cauliflower, cut into florets
- ¼ cup onion, thinly sliced
- 6 black olives, sliced

**For the marinade:**
- 1 tsp. olive oil
- Zest of 1 lemon
- Juice of 1 lemon
- 2 cloves garlic, minced
- 1 tsp. salt
- ½ tsp. pepper

1. In a 9"x 13" baking dish, distribute the rosemary and sun-dried tomatoes evenly on the bottom of the pan. Place the chicken on top.
2. In a medium bowl, stir together the oil, lemon zest, lemon juice, garlic, salt, and pepper. Pour the mixture over the chicken and place the dish in the refrigerator to marinate for at least 2 hours.
3. Preheat oven to 400°. Evenly distribute the onion, cauliflower, and olives over the chicken. Bake for 50-55 minutes and serve with additional chopped rosemary if desired.

☒ 3 oz of protein  
☐ 1 serving of fruit  
☒ 2 servings of vegetables  
☒ 1-2 servings of healthy fat

# Bruschetta Chicken

- ✓ 3 oz. chicken breast
- ✓ Salt and pepper to taste
- ✓ 1 cup tomatoes, chopped
- ✓ 1 clove garlic, minced
- ✓ 1 cup red onion, chopped
- ✓ 1 tsp. olive oil
- ✓ 1 tsp. balsamic vinegar
- ✓ ⅛ tsp. salt
- ✓ Handful basil, chopped

---

1. Preheat oven to 375°. Put chicken into baking dish and sprinkle with salt and pepper.
2. Combine remaining ingredients in a bowl and set aside.
3. Cover and bake chicken for about 35 to 40 minutes until juices run clear.
4. Spoon remaining ingredients over chicken and serve.

☒ 3 oz of protein  ☐ 1 serving of fruit

☒ 2 servings of vegetables  ☒ 1-2 servings of healthy fat

# Spinach Stuffed Salmon

- ✓ 3 oz. salmon, skin-on fillet
- ✓ 1 tsp. coconut oil
- ✓ ½ cup green onions, chopped
- ✓ ½ cup mushrooms, chopped
- ✓ 1 tsp. salt
- ✓ 1 tsp. black pepper
- ✓ 6 slivered almonds
- ✓ 1 cup spinach, chopped
- ✓ Few gratings whole nutmeg

1. Heat oil in a skillet over medium-high heat. Add green onions, mushrooms, salt, and pepper and sauté until soft and golden, about 3-4 minutes.
2. Add slivered almonds and continue cooking until slightly toasted, 1-2 minutes, then toss in spinach and cook until wilted, about 30 seconds.
3. Set aside to cool for 5-10 minutes, then stir in nutmeg.
4. Make an incision lengthwise in the salmon fillet, without going all the way through. The skin must remain intact.
5. Sprinkle with salt and pepper and stuff the fillet, packing as much as you can down the incision and mounding the rest on top of the fillet.
6. Delicately add the fillet to an oven-safe skillet, skin side down.
7. Cook uncovered for about 1 minute to sear the skin, then turn heat to low and cook for 5-8 minutes.
8. Transfer to oven and broil for about 2-3 minutes, until top turns golden and starts to bubble.

☒ 3 oz of protein☐ 1 serving of fruit

☒ 2 servings of vegetables☒ 1-2 servings of healthy fat

# Chicken, Broccoli and Squash Noodles

- 3 oz. chicken breast, cooked and sliced
- ½ cup broccoli florets
- 1 tsp. coconut oil
- ¼ cup cherry tomatoes, diced
- Juice and zest of 1 lemon
- 1 clove garlic, minced
- ½ tsp. oregano
- ¼ tsp. crushed red pepper
- Salt and pepper to taste
- 1¼ cups zucchini or yellow squash, spiralized
- 1 Tbsp. fresh parsley, chopped

---

1. Boil or steam the broccoli florets until tender, then drain and set aside.
2. Heat oil in a pan over medium heat. Add cherry tomatoes, lemon juice and zest, garlic, and spices and sauté for 1-2 minutes.
3. Add the zucchini/yellow squash noodles and sauté until desired tenderness.
4. Add zucchini/yellow squash mixture, broccoli, and chicken to a bowl and combine. Garnish with parsley.

☒ 3 oz of protein  ☐ 1 serving of fruit

☒ 2 servings of vegetables  ☒ 1-2 servings of healthy fat

# Salmon Zucchini Bowl

- ✓ 3 oz. salmon fillet
- ✓ 1 Tbsp. Braggs Liquid Aminos
- ✓ 1 small clove garlic, crushed
- ✓ 1½ cups zucchini, spiralized
- ✓ 1 tsp. coconut oil
- ✓ 2 Tbsp. water
- ✓ ½ cup baby spinach
- ✓ Salt to taste
- ✓ Pepper to taste

---

1. In a shallow dish, mix Braggs Liquid Aminos and garlic. Add salmon and turn fillet a few times to coat, leaving flesh side down to marinate for 10 minutes or so.

2. Heat oil in a large nonstick skillet over medium heat. Add marinated salmon and cook for 4-5 minutes or until golden crispy on each side. Transfer onto platter and set aside.

3. To the same skillet, add water, zucchini noodles, and spinach, cooking until desired doneness.

4. Transfer vegetables to a bowl and put salmon on top. Add salt and pepper to taste.

☒ 3 oz of protein ☐ 1 serving of fruit

☒ 2 servings of vegetables ☒ 1-2 servings of healthy fat

# Turkey and Kale Stew

- ✓ 1 large onion, finely chopped
- ✓ 5 cloves garlic, minced
- ✓ 1 tsp. olive oil
- ✓ 1 lb. ground turkey
- ✓ 14-oz. can diced tomatoes
- ✓ 1-2 cups water or stock
- ✓ 2 tsp. oregano or thyme
- ✓ ¾ tsp. salt
- ✓ ½ tsp. black pepper
- ✓ 2 bay leaves
- ✓ Juice of half a lemon
- ✓ ¾ cup Kalamata olives, halved
- ✓ 4 cups kale, coarsely chopped and packed
- ✓ ½ cup fresh basil, chopped
- ✓ ½ cup fresh parsley, chopped

1. Heat oil in a Dutch oven or large heavy-bottomed pot over medium heat. Add onion and garlic and sauté for 5 minutes or until translucent. Add turkey and brown well.
2. Add diced tomatoes, water/stock, oregano/thyme, salt, pepper, and bay leaves, then stir and bring to a boil. Reduce heat to low, cover, and simmer for 20 minutes.
3. Turn off heat and add lemon juice, olives, and kale, then stir, cover, and let stand a few minutes or until kale is wilted.
4. Stir in basil and parsley and let sit another 10 minutes. Discard the bay leaves and serve hot.
5. Makes 5 servings. 1 serving = 1½-2 cups

☒ 3 oz of protein  ☐ 1 serving of fruit

☒ 2 servings of vegetables  ☒ 1-2 servings of healthy fat

# Slow Cooker Blackberry Chicken

- ✓ 1 medium white onion, sliced into rings
- ✓ 1 lb. boneless, skinless chicken breasts
- ✓ 1 cup fresh blackberries
- ✓ ½ cup balsamic vinegar
- ✓ 2 tsp. garlic powder
- ✓ 1 tsp. dried rosemary
- ✓ Salt and pepper to taste after cooking

---

1. Layer the ingredients in your slow cooker in the order listed.
2. Cook on low for 4-6 hours.  Add salt and pepper to taste.
3. Makes 5 servings.  1 serving = 3 oz. chicken


☒ 3 oz of protein        ☐ 1 serving of fruit

☐ 2 servings of vegetables    ☐ 1-2 servings of healthy fat

# Lemon Almond Chicken Salad

- ✓ 3 oz. cooked, shredded chicken
- ✓ ½ cup onion, finely chopped
- ✓ 6 slivered or chopped almonds
- ✓ 1 tsp. garlic powder
- ✓ 1 tsp. cumin
- ✓ 1 tsp. coriander
- ✓ Juice of 1 lemon

---

Place all ingredients in a bowl and stir until well combined.

☒ 3 oz of protein ☐ 1 serving of fruit

☐ 2 servings of vegetables ☒ 1-2 servings of healthy fat

# Avocado Salmon Cakes

- ✓ 2 oz. canned salmon
- ✓ ⅛ avocado, mashed
- ✓ 1 egg, beaten
- ✓ 1 tsp. lemon juice
- ✓ ½ tsp. dill
- ✓ 1 tsp. coconut oil
- ✓ Salt and pepper to taste
- ✓ 2 cups fresh greens

---

1. Preheat oven to 350°. Line a baking sheet with parchment paper and set aside.
2. Combine salmon, avocado, egg, lemon juice, and dill in a bowl and mix until thickened.
3. Heat oil in a nonstick pan over medium-low heat. Form the mixture into a patty and place on the pan. Cook for 2-3 minutes per side or until browned, turning with a spatula. Transfer the patties to the baking sheet and bake for 8-10 minutes.
4. Serve with 2 cups fresh greens.

- ☒ 3 oz of protein
- ☒ 2 servings of vegetables
- ☐ 1 serving of fruit
- ☒ 1-2 servings of healthy fat

# Appetizers

Appetizers can add a sense of elegance to any meal or as a small plate dinner option for pizzazz.

"Once you start making changes, no matter how small, suddenly everything seems possible."

Oprah Winfrey

# Creamy Lemon Basil Spaghetti Squash

**Creamy Lemon Basil Sauce:**

(Makes 1 cup but 1 serving = 1 tsp.)
- ✓ ½ cup avocado, mashed
- ✓ 6 cloves garlic
- ✓ 1 cup fresh basil leaves
- ✓ 1 Tbsp. lemon zest
- ✓ ⅓ cup lemon juice
- ✓ ¼ cup olive oil
- ✓ ⅛ tsp. cayenne pepper (optional)
- ✓ ½ tsp. black pepper
- ✓ ½ tsp. salt

**Spaghetti Squash:**
- ✓ 1 tsp. coconut oil
- ✓ 1 cup spaghetti squash, cooked and cubed
- ✓ ½ cup kale, chopped
- ✓ ½ cup cherry tomatoes
- ✓ ½ tsp. black pepper
- ✓ ½ tsp. salt

---

1. Place all the sauce ingredients in a food processor or blender and purée until smooth.
2. Heat oil in a large skillet over medium-high heat. Add tomatoes and sauté for a few minutes.
3. Add the rest of the ingredients and sauté for another 5 minutes. Add 1 tsp. of sauce and mix thoroughly.

☐ 3 oz of protein   ☐ 1 serving of fruit

☒ 2 servings of vegetables   ☒ 1-2 servings of healthy fat

# Lime Basil Grilled Zucchini

- ✓ 2 small zucchini or 1 large zucchini
- ✓ 2 tsp. olive oil, divided
- ✓ Juice of 1 lime
- ✓ ¾ tsp. salt
- ✓ Black pepper to taste
- ✓ Handful of fresh basil, finely chopped

---

1. Preheat grill.
2. Cut zucchini lengthwise in half and then each half one more time. Drizzle 1 tsp. oil and put on a plate.
3. In a small bowl, whisk together 1 tsp. olive oil, lime juice, salt, pepper, and basil.
4. Preheat grill and cook zucchini until cooked but still firm, turning a few times.
5. Cut cooked zucchini into 1" pieces, add to a medium bowl, drizzle with sauce and gently mix. Serve warm or cold.

☐ 3 oz of protein                ☐ 1 serving of fruit

☒ 2 servings of vegetables       ☒ 1-2 servings of healthy fat

# Stuffed Portobello Mushrooms

- ✓ 2 medium Portobello mushrooms
- ✓ 2 tsp. olive oil, divided
- ✓ ¼ cup balsamic vinegar
- ✓ 3 oz. chicken, diced
- ✓ Salt and pepper to 2 cloves garlic, crushed
- ✓ ½ cup onion, finely diced
- ✓ 1 cup fresh spinach
- ✓ ½ cup grape tomatoes
- ✓ ¼ cup fresh basil, chopped
- ✓ Taste

1. Preheat oven to 350°.
2. Clean mushrooms and remove stems (save for later).
3. In a small bowl, whisk together 1 tsp. oil and balsamic vinegar. Pour the mixture into a large ziploc bag and add the mushrooms and mix to coat. Refrigerate up to 30 minutes.
4. Remove mushrooms and place them on a baking sheet. Bake for 15 minutes.
5. Meanwhile, heat 1 tsp. oil in a skillet over medium heat. Add garlic, chopped mushroom stems, and onion and let sauté for 5 minutes, stirring often.
6. Add in chicken, spinach, and roasted tomato and let cook for an additional 5 minutes.
7. After baking, pour any excess liquid from the mushrooms.
8. Spoon filling into each mushroom cap and serve.

☒ 3 oz of protein  ☐ 1 serving of fruit

☒ 2 servings of vegetables  ☒ 1-2 servings of healthy fat

# Tomato and Eggplant Ragout

- ½ cup tomatoes, diced
- ½ cup eggplant, cubed
- 2 cloves garlic, crushed
- 2 tsp. olive oil
- ¼ tsp. crushed red pepper
- ½ tsp. garlic powder
- ½ tsp. onion powder
- ½ tsp. Italian seasoning
- Salt and pepper to taste
- 1 cup spinach, chopped

---

1. Heat oil in a large skillet over medium heat. Add eggplant and garlic and sauté for 7 minutes, stirring frequently.
2. Add tomatoes and spices and let cook for 5 minutes. Reduce heat, add spinach, and let simmer for 15 minutes.
3. Serve with fish or chicken.

☐ 3 oz of protein  ☐ 1 serving of fruit

☒ 2 servings of vegetables  ☒ 1-2 servings of healthy fat

# Balsamic Chicken Zoodle Soup

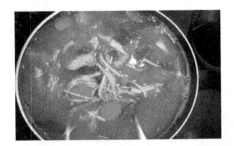

- ✓ 2 tsp. olive oil
- ✓ ⅓ cup onion, chopped
- ✓ ⅓ cup red bell pepper, chopped
- ✓ ⅓ cup butternut squash, chopped
- ✓ ½ tsp. garlic powder
- ✓ 2 tsp. oregano
- ✓ 1½ tsp. salt
- ✓ ¼ cup balsamic vinegar
- ✓ 3-4 cups low-sodium chicken stock/bone broth
- ✓ 1 bay leaf
- ✓ 3 oz. cooked, shredded chicken
- ✓ 1 cup zucchini, spiralized

1. Heat oil in a large soup pot or Dutch oven over medium-high heat. Add onions and sauté for 2 minutes, then add bell pepper and squash and sauté for another 2 minutes.
2. Add garlic, oregano, salt, balsamic vinegar, broth, and bay leaf. Cover and simmer for 20-25 minutes or until squash is tender.
3. Meanwhile, combine zucchini noodles and chicken in a bowl.
4. When ready, pour soup over noodles and chicken and serve.

☒ 3 oz of protein    ☐ 1 serving of fruit

☒ 2 servings of vegetables    ☒ 1-2 servings of healthy fat

# Stuffed Mushrooms

- ✓ 2 large white mushrooms, stems removed (save for later)
- ✓ ½ cup red bell pepper, finely chopped
- ✓ ½ cup large green bell pepper, finely chopped
- ✓ 1 tsp. olive oil
- ✓ 2 cloves garlic, minced
- ✓ ½ tsp. onion powder
- ✓ 2 oz. cooked turkey
- ✓ 1 egg
- ✓ ¼ cup tomato sauce

---

1. Preheat oven to 350°. Line a baking sheet with parchment paper and set aside.
2. Clean mushrooms and remove and chop the stems.
3. Mix all ingredients (including mushroom stems, but not mushroom caps) in a bowl.
4. Place mushroom caps on the baking sheet, and gently spoon filling into them.
5. Bake for 20-30 minutes, or until mushrooms are golden brown.

☒ 3 oz of protein   ☐ 1 serving of fruit

☒ 2 servings of vegetables   ☒ 1-2 servings of healthy fat

# Rosemary Roasted Almonds

- ✓ 1 Tbsp. butter
- ✓ 2 cups raw almonds
- ✓ 2 Tbsp. rosemary
- ✓ 2 tsp. salt
- ✓ ¼ tsp. black pepper

---

1. Melt butter in large skillet over medium-low heat.
2. When the butter starts bubbling, add almonds in a single layer and stir until coated.
3. Add rosemary, salt, and pepper.
4. Toast the almonds for 8-12 minutes, stirring often, until slightly darkened and aromatic.
5. Remove almonds and place on paper towel to cool.
6. 1 serving = 6 almonds

☐ 3 oz of protein  ☐ 1 serving of fruit

☐ 2 servings of vegetables  ☒ 1-2 servings of healthy fat

# Zucchini Chips

- ✓ 4 large zucchini, sliced ⅛" thick
- ✓ 2 Tbsp. avocado oil
- ✓ Salt
- ✓ ½ tsp. hot smoked paprika (optional)
- ✓ ½ tsp. cumin (optional)

---

1. Preheat oven to 235°. Lay zucchini slices on paper towels in a single layer. Cover with more paper towels and set a baking sheet on top of the zucchini slices. Press down to squeeze out some moisture.
2. Line several baking sheets with parchment paper. Brush parchment paper lightly with avocado oil and lay the zucchini slices in a single layer on the parchment paper. Fit as many on each baking sheet as possible. Lightly brush the top of the zucchini with avocado oil and sprinkle with salt. Sprinkle with a little cumin and smoked paprika if desired.
3. Bake for 1½–2 hours until crisp and golden. Remove the crisp chips and place any damp chips back in the oven for a few more minutes. Allow zucchini chips to cool on paper towels to absorb any extra oil.
4. 1 serving = 1 cup

- ☐ 3 oz of protein
- ☒ 2 servings of vegetables
- ☐ 1 serving of fruit
- ☒ 1-2 servings of healthy fat

# Butternut Squash Soup with Coconut Milk and Cilantro

- ✓ Flesh of 2 baked butternut squash
- ✓ 2 cups chicken broth
- ✓ 14-oz. can light, unsweetened coconut milk
- ✓ 2 tsp. dried cilantro
- ✓ 1 tsp. ground ginger
- ✓ Salt to taste
- ✓ Fresh cilantro, chopped

---

1. Place squash, chicken broth, coconut milk, dried cilantro, and ginger in a large soup pot and blend with a hand blender. Heat on the stovetop.
2. Serve and garnish with fresh cilantro.
3. Makes 3-4 servings. Serving size = 2 cups

☐ 3 oz of protein ☐ 1 serving of fruit

☒ 2 servings of vegetables ☒ 1-2 servings of healthy fat

# Spicy Salmon and Cucumber Bites

- ¼ cup Vegenaise
- ¼ tsp. smoked paprika
- ¼ tsp. hot sauce
- 6 oz. cooked salmon
- 1 Tbsp. shallots, minced
- 1 Tbsp. chives, chopped
- Salt and pepper to taste
- 1 English cucumber, peeled and cut into ¾" slices
- 4 cherry tomatoes, quartered
- 1 bunch chive sprigs (optional)

1. Combine Vegenaise, smoked paprika, and hot sauce in a small bowl and mix thoroughly.
2. Flake salmon into large bite-sized pieces. Place the salmon, shallots, chives, salt, and pepper in a bowl, add the Vegenaise mixture, and gently combine. Set aside.
3. Use a melon baller or small spoon to make a well in the center of each cucumber slice.
4. Spoon the salmon mixture into each cucumber slice and top each with a cherry tomato quarter and a couple of chive sprigs as desired.
5. Makes 2 servings.

☒ 3 oz of protein   ☐ 1 serving of fruit

☒ 2 servings of vegetables   ☒ 1-2 servings of healthy fat

# Red Cabbage Steaks

- ✓ 1 red cabbage
- ✓ 1 tsp. olive oil
- ✓ 1 Tbsp. garlic, minced
- ✓ 1 tsp. salt
- ✓ 1 tsp. black pepper
- ✓ ½ cup balsamic vinegar

---

1. Preheat oven to 425°.
2. Slice the cabbage steaks ½" thick starting from the top all the way through the bottom, leaving the core in.
3. Lay the "steaks" on a baking sheet and sprinkle with olive oil, garlic, salt, and pepper.
4. Bake for 20-25 minutes.
5. While the steaks are cooking, heat balsamic vinegar in a saucepan over medium-high heat. Lightly simmer until mixture has reduced by half.
6. Drizzle the reduction on the steaks before serving.

- ☐ 3 oz of protein
- ☒ 2 servings of vegetables
- ☐ 1 serving of fruit
- ☒ 1-2 servings of healthy fat

# Balsamic Chicken and Strawberry Skewers

- ✓ 3 oz. boneless, skinless chicken breast, cubed
- ✓ 1 tsp. salt
- ✓ 1 tsp. black pepper
- ✓ 1 tsp. olive oil
- ✓ ¼ cup balsamic vinegar
- ✓ 1 cup strawberries

1. Place the chicken, salt, pepper, and oil in a gallon-sized zip lock bag.
2. Measure the vinegar into a separate bowl or cup, and then pour half into the Ziploc bag. Reserve the rest in the bowl for later.
3. Seal the bag and shake to evenly coat the chicken. Let the chicken marinate in the refrigerator for 2-4 hours.
4. When ready to cook, place the strawberries in a bowl and pour in the reserved vinegar.
5. Line a baking sheet with parchment paper and assemble skewers by alternating chicken and strawberries and placing them on the baking sheet.
6. Broil the chicken on high, turning occasionally until the chicken is cooked thoroughly.
7. Heat remaining marinades from chicken and strawberries in a small pan over medium-low heat. Let the marinade reduce by at least half while the chicken cooks, whisking occasionally. Adjust the heat as needed to keep the reduction at a steady simmer.
8. Drizzle reduction over the skewers and serve.

☒ 3 oz of protein  ☐ 1 serving of fruit

☒ 2 servings of vegetables  ☒ 1-2 servings of healthy fat

# Entrées

Nourishing meals sustain our body and give us the energy we need to thrive in our daily life.

"Let food be thy medicine and medicine be thy food."

Hippocrates

# Sheet Pan Chicken Dinner

- ½ cup zucchini, sliced
- ⅓ cup asparagus, bite-sized pieces
- ½ cup butternut squash, bite-sized pieces
- ⅓ cup Brussels sprouts, halved or quartered Brussels
- ⅓ cup red onion, sliced thinly
- 4 cloves garlic, crushed
- 3 oz. chicken breast
- 2 tsp. olive oil

**Spice Mix:**
- 1 tsp. cumin
- 1 tsp. garlic powder
- 1 tsp. onion powder
- 1½ tsp. paprika
- 1 tsp. fresh thyme
- ¼ tsp. ground ginger
- Pinch cayenne pepper
- 1 tsp. salt
- 1 tsp. black pepper
- 4 thyme sprigs

---

1. Preheat oven to 400°. Line a baking sheet with parchment paper and set aside.
2. In a bowl, combine all veggies and garlic.
3. Add in halved chicken breast.
4. Pour oil, spices, and thyme sprigs over chicken mixture and coat evenly.
5. Transfer to baking sheet and bake for 25-30 minutes until chicken is fully cooked through. If chicken is done before vegetables, remove chicken and let veggies continue to cook.
6. Add additional salt and pepper as desired.

☒ 3 oz of protein  ☐ 1 serving of fruit

☒ 2 servings of vegetables  ☒ 1-2 servings of healthy fat

# Italian Style Spaghetti Squash Bake

- ✓ 1 spaghetti squash, halved and seeded
- ✓ 9 oz. shredded chicken breast
- ✓ 3 cups fresh spinach
- ✓ 1 tsp. olive oil
- ✓ 1 Tbsp. coconut oil
- ✓ 1 clove garlic, crushed
- ✓ 1 cup tomato sauce
- ✓ 1 egg, beaten
- ✓ 1½ Tbsp. Italian seasoning
- ✓ ½ tsp. crushed red pepper, more to taste
- ✓ 1 Tbsp. garlic powder
- ✓ ½ tsp. black pepper
- ✓ ¼ tsp. salt

1. Preheat oven to 375°. Line baking pan with tin foil and grease with olive oil.
2. Place spaghetti squash halves on the baking sheet, open side down, and bake for about 30 minutes.
3. Leaving the oven on, take out squash and use a fork to scrape out noodle strands into a bowl and set aside.
4. Heat coconut oil and garlic in a pan over medium heat. Add spinach and sauté.
5. In a glass baking dish, combine tomato sauce, egg, and spices. Add spaghetti squash, chicken, and spinach.
6. Sprinkle with crushed red pepper.
7. Bake for 10 minutes, then broil on high for 5 minutes or until top is crispy.
8. Makes 3 servings.

☒ 3 oz of protein  ☐ 1 serving of fruit

☒ 2 servings of vegetables  ☒ 1-2 servings of healthy fat

# Chicken Fajita Roll-Ups

**For the Marinade:**
- 2 Tbsp. olive oil
- Juice of half a lime
- 1 clove garlic, minced
- 1 tsp. chili powder
- ½ tsp. cumin
- ½ tsp. oregano
- ½ tsp. salt
- Pinch of cayenne pepper
- 2 Tbsp. cilantro, chopped

**For the chicken:**
- 3 chicken breasts or 6 thin, 3-oz., sliced chicken cutlets ¼" thick
- ½ red bell pepper, sliced
- ½ yellow bell pepper, sliced
- ½ green bell pepper, sliced

1. In a small bowl, whisk together oil, lime juice, garlic, chili powder, cumin, oregano, salt, cayenne, and cilantro. Set aside.
2. Slice chicken breasts lengthwise into 2 even slices and firmly pound the chicken using the smooth side of a meat tenderizer to an even ¼" thickness.
3. Place chicken cutlets into a large Ziploc bag and pour in marinade, making sure they are completely coated. Allow chicken to marinate for 1 hour overnight.
4. When ready to assemble, preheat oven to 375°. Evenly place six bell pepper slices of different colors in the middle of each chicken cutlet, roll up, and secure with a toothpick. Place seam side down in a lightly greased baking dish.
5. Brush tops of chicken with remaining marinade and bake for about 25-30 minutes or until the juices run clear.
6. Makes 6 servings.

- ☒ 3 oz of protein
- ☐ 1 serving of fruit
- ☒ 2 servings of vegetables
- ☒ 1-2 servings of healthy fat

# Balsamic and Herb Chicken

- ✓ 2 Tbsp. balsamic vinegar
- ✓ 2 tsp. Dijon mustard
- ✓ 1 clove garlic, minced
- ✓ ½ tsp. fresh thyme
- ✓ ⅛ tsp. cayenne
- ✓ Salt and pepper to taste
- ✓ 3 oz. boneless, skinless chicken breast
- ✓ 1 tsp. olive or coconut oil

---

1. In small bowl, whisk together balsamic vinegar, mustard, garlic, thyme, cayenne, salt, and pepper. Pour sauce into a large Ziploc bag and add chicken breast. Marinate the chicken for 30 minutes-12 hours.
2. Heat oil in a large skillet over medium-high heat. Transfer chicken to the skillet, cooking for 7-8 minutes per side, until golden brown and inside temperature is 165°.
3. Remove chicken and place on a cutting board to rest, then pour the remaining marinade into the heated skillet. Scrape up any brown bits and simmer, stirring occasionally.
4. Add chicken back into the skillet, coating well.

☒ 3 oz of protein ☐ 1 serving of fruit

☐ 2 servings of vegetables ☒ 1-2 servings of healthy fat

# Pan Roasted Blood Orange Chicken

- ✓ 3 oz. boneless, skinless chicken breast
- ✓ 1 Tbsp. garlic powder
- ✓ 1 Tbsp. chili powder
- ✓ 1 Tbsp. oregano
- ✓ 1 Tbsp. cumin
- ✓ 2 tsp. black pepper
- ✓ 2 tsp. salt
- ✓ Zest of 1 blood orange
- ✓ 1 tsp. olive oil
- ✓ Blood orange slices

1. Preheat oven to 425°.
2. Mix all the spices, zest, and oil in a bowl. Add chicken and thoroughly coat.
3. Place the chicken in an oven-safe skillet and top with orange slices.
4. Roast for 30 minutes or until chicken temperature reaches 165°.

☒ 3 oz of protein ☐ 1 serving of fruit

☐ 2 servings of vegetables ☒ 1-2 servings of healthy fat

# Charamoula Cod

- ✓ 1 tsp. avocado oil
- ✓ 2 Tbsp. lemon juice
- ✓ ½ Tbsp. paprika
- ✓ ½ Tbsp. cumin
- ✓ ½ Tbsp. garlic powder
- ✓ 1 Tbsp. dried parsley
- ✓ 1 Tbsp. dried cilantro
- ✓ 3 oz. cod

---

1. Preheat oven to 350°.
2. Mix all the ingredients (except the cod) in a small mixing bowl.
3. Grease a baking dish, add the cod, and spread the sauce evenly over the fish.
4. Bake until fish is cooked as desired.

☒ 3 oz of protein
☐ 1 serving of fruit
☐ 2 servings of vegetables
☒ 1-2 servings of healthy fat

# Chicken/Beef Apple Stuffed Acorn Squash

- ✓ 1 small acorn squash, halved and seeded
- ✓ 1 tsp. coconut oil
- ✓ 3 oz. ground beef or chicken
- ✓ 2 cups baby bella mushrooms, sliced
- ✓ 1 green apple, peeled and diced
- ✓ 6 silvered almonds

**Spice Mix:**
- ✓ 2 tsp. salt
- ✓ ½ tsp. black pepper
- ✓ ¼ tsp. garlic powder
- ✓ ½ tsp. thyme
- ✓ ½ tsp. sage
- ✓ ⅛ tsp. nutmeg

---

1. Preheat oven to 375°. Line a baking sheet with parchment and grease with oil.
2. Place squash halves on the baking sheet, open side down. Bake for about 30 minutes.
3. When the squash has 10 minutes left to cook, heat oil in a pan over medium heat. Add mushrooms and sauté for 1-2 minutes.
4. Add ground meat to the pan, season with the spice mix, and brown 3-5 minutes until almost cooked.
5. When meat is almost cooked, add the apples and cook an additional 2 minutes (apples should still be crisp).
6. Remove squash from the oven and fill the cavity of each squash half with the meat and apple mixture. Garnish with slivered almonds and serve.

☒ 3 oz of protein  ☒ 1 serving of fruit

☒ 2 servings of vegetables  ☒ 1-2 servings of healthy fat

# Stuffed Peppers

**Marinara Sauce:**
- 28-oz. can diced tomatoes
- 6-oz. can tomato paste
- 2 tsp. basil
- 1 tsp. oregano
- Salt and pepper to taste

**Peppers:**
- 5 large bell peppers
- 2 Tbsp. coconut oil
- 1 stalk celery, diced
- 3 cups riced cauliflower
- 4 oz. mushrooms, sliced
- 1-2 cloves garlic, minced
- 1 lb. ground beef
- 1 Tbsp. Italian seasoning
- 1 handful fresh sage, basil, or thyme
- Salt and pepper to taste

---

1. Preheat oven to 375°. Cut the tops off the peppers and remove seeds and ribs (save the tops). Fill a large soup pot partially with water and bring to a boil. Add peppers and parboil for 2-3 minutes.
2. Remove peppers and set aside in a glass baking dish. Fill the bottom of the baking dish with ½ cup water.
3. While the water boils, heat oil in a pan over medium heat. Stir in the riced cauliflower, celery, garlic, and mushrooms. Sauté about 5 minutes, remove the vegetables from the pan, and set aside.
4. Add ground beef to the pan and lightly brown. Add the vegetables back to the pan, add all the seasonings, and stir together.

5. Stuff the filling evenly into the peppers, replace the tops back on the peppers, and bake for 30-35 minutes.

6. While the peppers bake, stir together all the marinara ingredients in a saucepan over medium heat. Bring to a light boil and then reduce to simmer for 15-20 minutes. Serve the peppers with marinara sauce.

7. Makes 5 servings. 1 serving = 1 stuffed pepper

☒ 3 oz of protein  ☐ 1 serving of fruit

☒ 2 servings of vegetables  ☒ 1-2 servings of healthy fat

# Creamy Butternut Squash Soup

- ✓ 1 head cauliflower, chopped
- ✓ 1 small butternut squash, diced
- ✓ 2 cloves garlic, minced
- ✓ 1 stalk celery, chopped
- ✓ 4 cups chicken broth
- ✓ 4-6 fresh sage leaves, chopped
- ✓ 2 Tbsp. coconut oil
- ✓ Salt and pepper to taste
- ✓ Scallions, sliced

_____

1. Heat oil in a large deep pan or soup pot. Add cauliflower and squash. Sauté 2-3 minutes, then add garlic, celery, and sage and sauté for another 2-3 minutes.
2. Pour 4 cups broth into the pot and bring to a low boil. Reduce to a simmer and cover for about 10 minutes, or until the vegetables are fork tender.
3. Use a slotted spoon to transfer about half the cauliflower florets to a separate bowl.
4. Pour the remaining soup into a blender in 2 batches, and blend until smooth. Return the soup to the pot and stir in the reserved cauliflower. Season with salt and pepper to taste.
5. Serve the soup into bowls and top with sliced scallions.
6. 1 serving = 2 cups

☐ 3 oz of protein   ☐ 1 serving of fruit

☒ 2 servings of vegetables   ☒ 1-2 servings of healthy fat

# Lime Chicken Kabobs

- ✓ 3 cloves garlic, minced
- ✓ ⅓ cup lime juice
- ✓ 2 Tbsp. olive oil
- ✓ ½ tsp. cumin
- ✓ ½ tsp. salt
- ✓ ½ tsp. black pepper
- ✓ 1 lb. chicken breasts, cut into 1" pieces
- ✓ Salt and pepper to taste
- ✓ Cilantro leaves, chopped (optional)

1. In a large bowl, mix garlic, lime juice, oil, cumin, salt, and pepper. Add chicken and stir until evenly coated.  Cover and refrigerate for 30 minutes-8 hours.
2. Preheat grill to medium-high heat.
3. Drain marinade from bowl.  Thread chicken onto skewers, then season the chicken with a few extra pinches of salt and pepper.  Place skewers on the grill and cook for 6-8 minutes, turning once, until the chicken is cooked through.  Garnish with fresh cilantro if desired.
4. Makes 5 servings.

☒ 3 oz of protein  ☐ 1 serving of fruit

☐ 2 servings of vegetables  ☒ 1-2 servings of healthy fat

# Korean Steak Kabobs

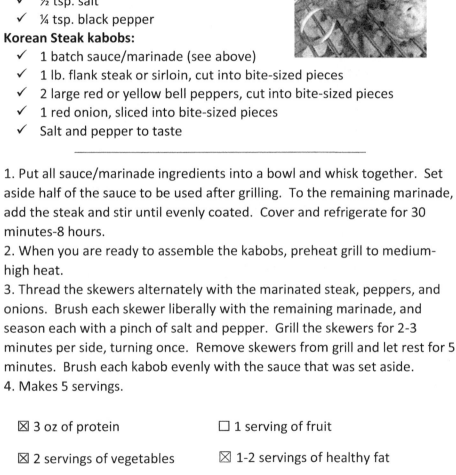

**Sauce/Marinade:**
- ¼ cup lemon, juiced and zested
- 1 Tbsp. olive oil
- 4 cloves garlic, minced
- 1 Tbsp. oregano
- ½ tsp. salt
- ¼ tsp. black pepper

**Korean Steak kabobs:**
- 1 batch sauce/marinade (see above)
- 1 lb. flank steak or sirloin, cut into bite-sized pieces
- 2 large red or yellow bell peppers, cut into bite-sized pieces
- 1 red onion, sliced into bite-sized pieces
- Salt and pepper to taste

---

1. Put all sauce/marinade ingredients into a bowl and whisk together. Set aside half of the sauce to be used after grilling. To the remaining marinade, add the steak and stir until evenly coated. Cover and refrigerate for 30 minutes-8 hours.
2. When you are ready to assemble the kabobs, preheat grill to medium-high heat.
3. Thread the skewers alternately with the marinated steak, peppers, and onions. Brush each skewer liberally with the remaining marinade, and season each with a pinch of salt and pepper. Grill the skewers for 2-3 minutes per side, turning once. Remove skewers from grill and let rest for 5 minutes. Brush each kabob evenly with the sauce that was set aside.
4. Makes 5 servings.

☒ 3 oz of protein                    ☐ 1 serving of fruit

☒ 2 servings of vegetables    ☒ 1-2 servings of healthy fat

# Zoodles Marinara

- ✓ 1 Tbsp. olive oil
- ✓ ½ cup white onion, diced
- ✓ 6 cloves garlic, minced
- ✓ 28-oz. can diced tomatoes
- ✓ 2 large zucchinis, spiralized
- ✓ ½ cup fresh basil leaves, roughly chopped
- ✓ 1½ tsp. salt
- ✓ ¼ tsp. black pepper
- ✓ ⅛ tsp. crushed red pepper

---

1. Heat oil in a large sauté pan over medium-high heat. Add onions and sauté for 5 minutes, then add garlic and sauté for 1 more minute.
2. Add tomatoes, tomato paste, basil, salt, pepper, and crushed red pepper, and stir to combine.
3. Continue cooking until the sauce reaches a simmer, then reduce heat to medium-low and continue to simmer for about 15 minutes.
4. Add in zucchini noodles and toss until evenly coated with sauce. Continue to cook for 2-3 minutes until the noodles are slightly softened.
5. 1 serving = 2 cups

☐ 3 oz of protein

☐ 1 serving of fruit

☒ 2 servings of vegetables

☒ 1-2 servings of healthy fat

# Coconut Crusted Cod

- ✓ 6 oz. cod
- ✓ 4 cups asparagus, trimmed
- ✓ 1 Tbsp. coconut oil
- ✓ ¼ cup coconut milk
- ✓ 6 Tbsp. shredded coconut
- ✓ 1 tsp. paprika
- ✓ 1 tsp. garlic powder
- ✓ Salt and pepper to taste

---

1. Preheat oven to 400°. Line a baking sheet with parchment paper and set aside.
2. Cover asparagus with melted oil and put in oven.
3. Add coconut milk to a shallow bowl.
4. In a separate shallow bowl, combine shredded coconut, paprika, garlic powder, salt, and pepper.
5. Soak the cod in the milk for 1 minute on each side. Dip in the shredded coconut mixture, coating both sides. Transfer fish to the baking sheet and bake for 12-15 minutes, until cooked through and flaky. When you put the fish in the oven, check the asparagus and assess how much longer it needs to bake.
6. Makes 2 servings

☒ 3 oz of protein ☐ 1 serving of fruit

☒ 2 servings of vegetables ☒ 1-2 servings of healthy fat

# Butternut Squash Noodle Hash

- 1 tsp. butter
- 1½ cups butternut squash, spiralized
- ½ cup kale, chopped
- ¼ tsp. ground ginger
- ½ tsp. onion powder
- ⅛-¼ tsp. crushed red pepper
- Salt and pepper to taste
- 1 Tbsp. Bragg's Liquid Aminos
- 2 eggs
- Fresh dill (optional)

---

1. Preheat oven to 400°.
2. Melt butter in an oven-safe skillet over medium heat. Add squash noodles and kale and season with ginger, onion powder, and crushed red pepper. Add salt and pepper to taste.
3. Sauté for about 5 minutes, stirring occasionally. Add the Bragg's Liquid Aminos, cover with a lid and cook for an additional 1-2 minutes, until the noodles are softened.
4. Flatten the noodles with the back of a spatula and make 2 wells with a spoon. Crack an egg into each well and transfer the skillet to the oven.
5. Bake for 6-8 minutes, until the egg whites are set.
6. Garnish with fresh dill as desired.

- ☒ 3 oz of protein
- ☒ 2 servings of vegetables
- ☐ 1 serving of fruit
- ☒ 1-2 servings of healthy fat

# Garlic Lover's Salmon

- ✓ 3 oz. salmon
- ✓ 1 tsp. butter
- ✓ 2 cloves garlic, roughly chopped
- ✓ 2 Tbsp. fresh lemon juice, plus extra lemon wedges for serving
- ✓ Salt and pepper to taste
- ✓ ¼ cup fresh Italian parsley, chopped
- ✓ ¼ cup green onions, thinly sliced

1. Preheat oven to 375° or a grill to medium heat. Line a baking dish with aluminum foil.
2. Melt butter in a small saucepan over medium-high heat. Stir in garlic and sauté for 1-2 minutes until not quite fully soft. Remove from heat and stir in the lemon juice.
3. Using a pastry brush, brush a Tbsp. of the garlic butter mixture on the foil until it is evenly covered. Place salmon on the foil and pour the remainder on the salmon and brush it until evenly covered. Season with a few generous pinches of salt and pepper.
4. Fold the sides of the aluminum foil over the salmon until it is completely enclosed.
5. Bake or grill for 10-15 minutes, depending on the thickness of the fish. Remove salmon from the oven or grill and pull back the aluminum foil so that the top of the fish is completely exposed. Continue grilling, or if in the oven, change setting to broil and continue cooking the fish for 3-4 minutes, or until the top of the salmon and the garlic are slightly golden and the fish is cooked through.
6. Garnish with parsley and green onions and serve with lemon wedges.

☒ 3 oz of protein      ☐ 1 serving of fruit

☐ 2 servings of vegetables      ☒ 1-2 servings of healthy fat

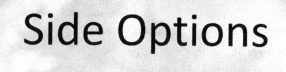

# Side Options

Side options to a meal can either complement or detract. These healthful and delicious side options are sure to add a complementary flavor to anything you serve.

"One cannot think well, love well, sleep well, if one has not dined well."

Virginia Woolf

# "Pasta" Salad

**For the noodles:**
- ✓ 1 large broccoli stem, spiralized
- ✓ 1 large zucchini, spiralized
- ✓ 2 yellow squash, spiralized
- ✓ 1 red onion, spiralized

**Everything else:**
- ✓ ½ cup roasted red peppers, finely chopped
- ✓ ¼ cup roasted garlic, finely chopped
- ✓ ½ cup broccoli florets, finely chopped

**Dressing:**
- ✓ 2 Tbsp. olive oil
- ✓ 1 Tbsp. Italian seasoning
- ✓ 1 ½ Tbsp. apple cider vinegar
- ✓ Juice of half a lemon
- ✓ ½ tsp. salt
- ✓ ½ tsp. black pepper
- ✓ ¼–½ tsp. crushed red pepper (optional)

---

1. Put all veggies in a bowl.
2. In a separate bowl, whisk together dressing ingredients. Pour over veggies and combine.
3. 1 serving = 2 cups vegetables and 1-2 tsp. of dressing

☐ 3 oz of protein  ☐ 1 serving of fruit

☒ 2 servings of vegetables  ☒ 1-2 servings of healthy fat

# Spanish Cauliflower Rice

- ✓ 1-2 tsp. coconut oil
- ✓ 2 cups riced cauliflower
- ✓ ¼ cup crushed tomatoes
- ✓ 2 tsp. garlic powder
- ✓ 2 tsp. onion powder
- ✓ 2 tsp. cumin
- ✓ 1 tsp. chili powder
- ✓ Salt to taste

---

1. Heat oil in a skillet over medium heat.
2. Add cauliflower and sauté until almost done, about 3-5 minutes.
3. Add tomatoes and spices and heat through.

☐ 3 oz of protein  
☒ 2 servings of vegetables  
☐ 1 serving of fruit  
☒ 1-2 servings of healthy fat

# Easy Roasted Eggplant

- ✓ 2 medium eggplants
- ✓ 12 cloves garlic
- ✓ 1 Tbsp. olive oil
- ✓ ¼ cup onion, chopped finely
- ✓ ¼ cup scallions, chopped (the green part)
- ✓ Salt and pepper to taste
- ✓ Hot pepper, chopped (optional)

---

1. Make six 1" slits around each eggplant, and stuff garlic in each slit and coat with oil.
2. Wrap with heavy foil. Add directly to burner and roast on low-medium heat for about 10 minutes on each side, until soft. Remove and let rest for 5 minutes.
3. Unwrap foil, halve the eggplant, and scoop out insides into a bowl.
4. Mix thoroughly to ensure garlic is mashed. Add onion, scallions, salt, and pepper.
5. 1 serving = 2 cups

☐ 3 oz of protein  ☐ 1 serving of fruit

☒ 2 servings of vegetables  ☒ 1-2 servings of healthy fat

# Sautéed Mushroom Berry Chard

- ✓ 2 tsp. olive oil
- ✓ 5 cloves garlic, minced
- ✓ ¼ cup onion, sliced
- ✓ 1 cup portobello mushrooms, sliced
- ✓ ¾ cup chard, chopped
- ✓ Salt to taste
- ✓ 1 cup fresh blueberries and/or raspberries

1. Heat oil in pan over medium heat and add garlic and onion. Sauté for about 2 minutes.
2. Add sliced mushrooms and sauté 5 more minutes.
3. Add chard and sauté for 2 more minutes until wilted. Do not overcook.
4. Add salt to taste.
5. Remove from heat and top with berries right before serving.

☐ 3 oz of protein  ☒ 1 serving of fruit

☒ 2 servings of vegetables  ☒ 1-2 servings of healthy fat

# Candied Butternut Squash

- ½ large butternut squash, peeled, seeded, and cut into 1" cubes
- 1 Tbsp. grapeseed oil
- 1 Tbsp. Stevia
- ½ tsp. cinnamon
- ½ tsp. nutmeg
- Butter

---

1. Preheat oven to 350°.
2. Combine the first five ingredients in a mixing bowl.
3. Lightly coat the bottom of a glass bowl or baking dish with butter and add the mixture.
4. Cover with foil and bake 30 minutes, then remove foil and bake at least another 30 minutes until tender.
5. 1 serving = 1 cup

☐ 3 oz of protein  ☐ 1 serving of fruit

☒ 2 servings of vegetables  ☒ 1-2 servings of healthy fat

# Grilled Leek and Roasted Bell Pepper Salsa

- ✓ 1 leek, trimmed
- ✓ 2 green bell peppers, whole
- ✓ 4 cups tomatoes, chopped
- ✓ 1 cup cilantro, chopped
- ✓ 1 Tbsp. garlic, minced
- ✓ 1 Tbsp. jalapeno, chopped
- ✓ ¼ cup lime
- ✓ 1 Tbsp. olive oil
- ✓ ½ tsp. black pepper, or to taste
- ✓ 1 tsp. salt, or to taste

1. Preheat grill to high.
2. Brush the leeks and bell peppers with oil.
3. Place leeks on the grill and roast for about 2-3 minutes each side.
4. Add the peppers and roast about 8-10 minutes. Periodically rotate the peppers to evenly char the skin.
5. Remove from heat and add peppers to a bowl and cover with plastic wrap and let sweat for about 8-10 minutes
6. Combine the tomato, cilantro, garlic, jalapeno, lime, pepper and salt in a large bowl.
7. Remove the outer layers of the leeks that are too charred. Slice the leek in half and then thinly slice. Add to the salsa.
8. Carefully scrape the charred skin of the bell peppers and discard. Seed and remove stems, chop, and add to salsa.
9. If you prefer less chunky salsa, use a blender or food processor.
10. Makes 3 servings. 1 serving = 2 cups

☐ 3 oz of protein   ☐ 1 serving of fruit

☒ 2 servings of vegetables   ☒ 1-2 servings of healthy fat

# Dijon and Apple Brussels Sprouts

- ✓ 1 tsp. olive oil
- ✓ 2 cups Brussels sprouts, quartered
- ✓ 2 cloves garlic, minced
- ✓ 1 green apple, peeled and diced
- ✓ ¼ cup Dijon mustard
- ✓ ½ cup bone broth or vegetable stock
- ✓ Zest of 1 lemon
- ✓ ⅛ tsp. cayenne pepper
- ✓ 1 tsp. salt
- ✓ 1 tsp. black pepper
- ✓ 6 slivered almonds

1. Preheat oven to 425°.
2. Heat oil in an oven-safe large skillet over medium-high heat.
3. Add Brussels sprouts and let sear for about 5 minutes. Add garlic and apple and cook 2-3 more minutes.
4. In a bowl, combine mustard, broth, lemon zest, cayenne, salt, and pepper, and add to the Brussels sprouts.
5. Place in the oven and bake for approximately 15 minutes, then turn the oven to broil and cook for another 3-4 minutes or until slightly crisp on top.
6. Remove from oven and top with the slivered almonds.

☐ 3 oz of protein

☒ 1 serving of fruit

☒ 2 servings of vegetables

☒ 1-2 servings of healthy fat

# Zesty Cauliflower Tabbouleh

- ✓ 1 head cauliflower, grated or riced
- ✓ 4 tomatoes, diced
- ✓ 1 cup cilantro, finely chopped
- ✓ ¼ cup lemon juice
- ✓ ¼ cup lime juice
- ✓ 2 tsp. garlic powder
- ✓ Salt and pepper to taste

---

1. Use a food processor or hand grater to process the cauliflower so that it resembles quinoa or rice. Transfer to a large mixing bowl.
2. Add in tomatoes and cilantro and combine.
3. Add lemon juice, lime juice, salt, pepper, and garlic powder. Mix well.
4. Makes 4 servings. 1 serving = 2 cups

☐ 3 oz of protein ☐ 1 serving of fruit

☒ 2 servings of vegetables ☐ 1-2 servings of healthy fat

# Grilled Veggie Platter

- ✓ 4 medium zucchinis, ½" slices
- ✓ 1 medium yellow squash
- ✓ 1 red bell pepper, sliced
- ✓ 1 yellow bell pepper, sliced
- ✓ 1 red onion, thinly sliced
- ✓ 1 lb. asparagus, ends trimmed
- ✓ 1 Tbsp. olive oil

**For the sauce:**
- ✓ ¼ cup Vegenaise
- ✓ Juice of 1 lime
- ✓ 2 cloves garlic, crushed
- ✓ 1 tsp. cumin
- ✓ Salt and pepper to taste

1. In a medium bowl, whisk together all the ingredients for the sauce and set aside.
2. Slice the zucchini and squash in half lengthwise and then into ½" slices. Preheat the grill to low heat. Lightly drizzle the vegetables with oil and toss to coat.
3. Working in batches, place the vegetables on the grill in a single layer. Close the lid and cook for 10-12 minutes, turning once. Transfer to a serving plate and serve with the sauce.
4. Makes 4-6 servings. 1 serving = 2 cups

☐ 3 oz of protein  ☐ 1 serving of fruit

☒ 2 servings of vegetables  ☒ 1-2 servings of healthy fat

# Creamy Cauliflower and Leek Soup

- ✓ 3 Tbsp. olive oil
- ✓ 2 large leeks, trimmed and medium chopped
- ✓ 2 stalks celery cleaned and medium chopped
- ✓ 3 cloves garlic, minced
- ✓ 1-quart vegetable stock
- ✓ 3 cups water
- ✓ 1 bay leaf
- ✓ 1 Tbsp. salt
- ✓ 1 tsp. black pepper
- ✓ 1 head cauliflower, cut into 2" florets
- ✓ 1½ tsp. apple cider vinegar
- ✓ Chives, finely chopped

---

1. Heat oil over medium-high heat in a large soup pot or Dutch oven. Add leeks, celery, and sauté about 5-6 minutes. Add the garlic and sauté another minute.
2. Add the stock, 2 cups water, bay leaf, salt & pepper, then bring to a boil.
3. Add the cauliflower florets and turn the heat to medium. Simmer 30 minutes until the cauliflower is fork tender. Discard the bay leaf. Purée the soup with a hand blender, or in small batches in a high-speed blender or food processor until smooth.
4. Add the soup back to the pot and stir in vinegar and 1 cup water (depending on desired texture).
5. Garnish with chives.
6. Makes 8-10 servings. 1 serving = 1 cup

☐ 3 oz of protein ☐ 1 serving of fruit

☒ 2 servings of vegetables ☒ 1-2 servings of healthy fat

# BBQ Zucchini

- ✓ 2 cups zucchini, quartered
- ✓ 1 Tbsp. garlic powder
- ✓ 1 Tbsp. onion powder
- ✓ ¼ tsp. salt
- ✓ ½ tsp. black pepper
- ✓ 2 tsp. olive oil

---

1. Preheat grill to medium.
2. Place all ingredients in a large Ziploc bag and combine until the zucchini is coated.
3. Grill until zucchini is cooked to your liking, turning once.

☐ 3 oz of protein  ☐ 1 serving of fruit

☒ 2 servings of vegetables  ☒ 1-2 servings of healthy fat

# Curry Cauliflower

- ✓ 2 cups cauliflower, bite-sized pieces
- ✓ 2 tsp. olive oil
- ✓ 1-2 Tbsp. garlic powder to taste
- ✓ 1-2 Tbsp. onion powder to taste
- ✓ 1-2 Tbsp. curry powder to taste

---

1. Preheat oven to 350°.
2. Use half of the oil to grease baking sheet and add cauliflower in a single layer.
3. Drizzle the other half of the oil over the cauliflower.
4. Sprinkle spices over the cauliflower and put baking sheet in the oven.
5. Bake until the cauliflower has some golden edges and is easily pierced with a fork.

☐ 3 oz of protein  ☐ 1 serving of fruit

☒ 2 servings of vegetables  ☒ 1-2 servings of healthy fat

# Balsamic Glazed Meatballs

- ✓ 1 lb. ground beef
- ✓ 3 Tbsp. water
- ✓ 1 tsp. garlic powder
- ✓ 1 tsp. onion powder
- ✓ 1 Tbsp. parsley, divided

- ✓ Salt and pepper to taste

**For the reduction:**
- ✓ 1 cup balsamic vinegar
- ✓ 2 Tbsp. coconut oil

---

1. Preheat oven to 375°.
2. In saucepan, heat the balsamic vinegar over medium heat to bring to a slow boil (small bubbles). Whisk often until the vinegar reduces by half and thickens, about 15 minutes.
3. Stir the oil into the vinegar and remove from heat.
4. While vinegar is reducing, put ground beef in a large mixing bowl, and add garlic, onion, salt, pepper, and 2 tsp. of the parsley. Using your hands, also add the water and mix thoroughly. Form 16-20 meatballs.
5. Bake the meatballs for 10 minutes. Pour the reduction over the meatballs and return to the oven to finish cooking, about 5-8 minutes.
6. Sprinkle with the leftover tsp. of parsley and serve the meatballs, saving the excess reduction for dipping.
7. Makes 5 servings. 1 serving = 3 oz.

☒ 3 oz of protein  ☐ 1 serving of fruit

☐ 2 servings of vegetables  ☒ 1-2 servings of healthy fat

# Caramelized Onion Green Beans with Toasted Almonds

- ✓ 1½ cups green beans, trimmed
- ✓ ½ cup onion, thinly sliced
- ✓ 1 tsp. freshly grated garlic
- ✓ 1 tsp. butter
- ✓ 6 diced almonds
- ✓ Salt and pepper to taste

---

1. In a large saucepan, add water and bring to boil. Add green beans and cook for a few minutes until beans are crisp. Remove beans from water and place into an ice bath to blanch.
2. Melt butter in a large sauté pan over medium heat. Add onions and sauté 15 minutes or until caramelized.
3. Toast almonds in a small pan over medium heat about 5 minutes or until golden brown.
4. Add the caramelized onions to the green beans and season with salt and pepper. Top with toasted almonds.

- ☐ 3 oz of protein
- ☒ 2 servings of vegetables
- ☐ 1 serving of fruit
- ☒ 1-2 servings of healthy fat

# Herb Baked Butternut Squash

- ✓ 4 cups butternut squash, cubed
- ✓ 2 tsp. olive oil
- ✓ Juice of 1 lemon
- ✓ 2 cloves garlic, minced
- ✓ 1 tsp. marjoram
- ✓ 1 tsp. parsley
- ✓ 1 tsp. onion powder
- ✓ Salt and pepper to taste

---

1. Preheat oven to 350°. Line a baking sheet with parchment paper and set aside.
2. Cube the squash to desired size.
3. Put squash in a single layer on the baking sheet. Coat with oil and sprinkle the herbs and spices over the squash.
4. Bake until soft, about 30 minutes.
5. Makes 2 servings. 1 serving = 2 cups

☐ 3 oz of protein

☐ 1 serving of fruit

☒ 2 servings of vegetables

☒ 1-2 servings of healthy fat

# Salads

In the past, salads have gotten a bad rap. If you are creative with your salads, however, they can provide a bountiful abundance of beautiful colors and nutrition. Salads are not just pretty to look at but can be amazing to eat too.

"The beauty of life is in small details,
not big events."
Jim Jarmusch

# Burger Salad with Mustard Dressing

- ✓ 1 cup lettuce, chopped
- ✓ 2 oz. cooked burger
- ✓ ⅓ cup tomato, sliced
- ✓ ⅓ cup onion, diced
- ✓ 1 soft-boiled egg
- ✓ ⅓ cup poblano pepper, roasted and chopped

**For the Dressing:**
- ✓ 2 Tbsp. mustard
- ✓ 1 Tbsp. apple cider vinegar
- ✓ 2 tsp. olive oil
- ✓ ¼ tsp. pepper

---

1. Place lettuce in a large bowl.
2. Add burger, tomato, onion, and egg. Feel free to add other toppings.
3. In a small bowl, whisk together dressing ingredients.
4. Pour over salad and serve.


☒ 3 oz of protein   ☐ 1 serving of fruit

☒ 2 servings of vegetables   ☒ 1-2 servings of healthy fat

# Strawberry Chicken Spinach Salad with Citrus Dressing

- ⅓ cup red onion, sliced
- ⅓ cup cucumber, sliced
- 1 cup strawberries, chopped
- ⅓ cup roasted asparagus, chopped
- ⅛ avocado, chopped *or* 6-8 almonds, toasted
- 3 oz. cooked chicken breast
- 1 cup spinach

**Citrus dressing:**
- ½ cup fresh grapefruit juice
- Liquid Stevia to taste
- ½ tsp. salt
- ¼ tsp. black pepper
- 1 tsp. Dijon mustard
- 1 clove garlic, minced
- 1 tsp. olive oil

---

1. In a small bowl, whisk together all dressing ingredients.
2. Put salad ingredients in a bowl, add the dressing, and toss.

☒ 3 oz of protein

☒ 1 serving of fruit

☒ 2 servings of vegetables

☒ 1-2 servings of healthy fat

# Grilled Veggie and Chicken Salad with Tomato Vinaigrette

**For the chicken:**
- ✓ 3 oz. chicken breast
- ✓ 1 tsp. rosemary
- ✓ 1 tsp. Italian seasoning
- ✓ ¼ tsp. salt

**For the veggies:**
- ✓ ⅓ cup zucchini, sliced
- ✓ ⅓ cup yellow squash, sliced
- ✓ ⅓ cup red pepper, sliced
- ✓ ⅓ cup cherry tomatoes, quartered
- ✓ ⅓ cup red onion, sliced
- ✓ 1 tsp. olive oil
- ✓ 1 tsp. salt
- ✓ ⅓ cup spinach

**Tomato Vinaigrette:**
- ✓ ½ cup diced tomatoes, blended
- ✓ 1 Tbsp. apple cider vinegar
- ✓ Dash black pepper
- ✓ ½ tsp. garlic powder
- ✓ ½ tsp. onion powder
- ✓ 1 tsp. olive oil
- ✓ Dash fine salt
- ✓ ¼ tsp. cayenne (optional

---

1. Preheat grill to medium-high.
2. Toss chicken in spices and set aside.  Cut veggies, toss in oil, and salt, and set aside.
3. Spray the grill and heat to 350-400°.  Place the chicken breast on one side.  On the other side, place a layer of greased tin foil for the zucchini, squash, red pepper, tomatoes, and red onion.
4. Grill chicken for about 7-8 minutes on each side.  Grill veggies until desired doneness and make sure chicken is fully cooked.

5. Blend all vinaigrette ingredients in a blender until smooth.
6. Slice chicken and put veggies and chicken on top of a bed of spinach. Add dressing and serve.

☒ 3 oz of protein ☐ 1 serving of fruit

☒ 2 servings of vegetables ☒ 1-2 servings of healthy fat

# Blueberry, Kale and Butternut Squash Salad

- ½ cup kale, washed and ribs removed
- ¼ cup spring mix
- 1 cup blueberries
- 6 Kalamata olives, cut into slivers
- ¼ cup red or yellow bell pepper, thinly sliced
- 1 cup butternut squash, cubed
- 1 tsp. olive oil (divided)
- 1 Tbsp. balsamic vinegar
- ½ tsp. salt
- Black pepper to taste

_____

1. Preheat oven to 400°. Lightly grease a baking sheet.
2. Toss squash cubes in ½ tsp. olive oil and a pinch of salt and spread on the baking sheet.
3. Bake 30-40 minutes, turning once or twice until all the pieces are tender.
4. Remove the squash from oven when finished and let the squash cool.
5. Stack the kale leaves and roll them into tight bundles, then slice very thinly with a sharp knife to create shredded pieces.
6. In a salad bowl, whisk together dressing by combining oil, balsamic vinegar, salt, and pepper.
7. Add kale, spring mix, blueberries, olives, pepper, and squash, and toss everything together. Let the salad marinate in the refrigerator for 30 minutes to an hour before serving.

☐ 3 oz of protein          ☒ 1 serving of fruit

☒ 2 servings of vegetables     ☒ 1-2 servings of healthy fat

# Roasted Vegetable Salad with Shallot Vinaigrette

- ¼ cup asparagus spears, cut into 1½" pieces
- ¼ cup frozen artichoke hearts, thawed
- ¼ cup Roma tomatoes, sliced ½" thick
- 1 tsp. melted coconut oil
- Salt to taste
- 1 cup romaine lettuce, chopped
- ¼ cup roasted red bell pepper, chopped
- ⅛ ripe avocado, chopped

**Shallot Vinaigrette:**
- 2 Tbsp. apple cider vinegar
- 1 Tbsp. shallot, minced
- 1 tsp. olive oil
- 2 Tbsp. water
- 2 tsp. Dijon mustard
- 1 clove garlic, minced

1. Preheat oven to 350°, and line a baking sheet with parchment paper.
2. Combine the asparagus, artichoke hearts, and tomatoes in a large bowl and toss with the melted coconut oil.
3. Arrange the vegetables in a single layer on the baking sheet, sprinkle with salt, and roast in the oven until tender, about 30 minutes.
4. Add vinaigrette ingredients to a blender and blend until completely smooth.
5. In a large serving bowl, layer romaine, warm roasted vegetables, roasted pepper, and chopped avocado. Add dressing and toss salad.

☐ 3 oz of protein   ☐ 1 serving of fruit

☒ 2 servings of vegetables   ☒ 1-2 servings of healthy fat

# Strawberry Avocado Arugula Salad

- ✓ 2 cups arugula, or lettuce of choice
- ✓ 1 Tbsp. lemon juice
- ✓ 1 tsp. olive oil
- ✓ ⅛ avocado, diced
- ✓ 1 cup fresh strawberries, sliced
- ✓ 1 tsp. chopped fresh mint, plus more for garnish
- ✓ Pinch of lemon zest, plus more to taste
- ✓ Salt and pepper to taste

1. Toss the arugula in 1 Tbsp. lemon juice and oil.

2. In a separate bowl, gently toss the avocado with the strawberries, mint, and lemon zest. Arrange over the arugula.

3. Garnish with mint and salt and pepper to taste.

☐ 3 oz of protein

☒ 1 serving of fruit

☒ 2 servings of vegetables

☒ 1-2 servings of healthy fat

# Rosemary Grilled Chicken and Peach Salad

**Rosemary Grilled Chicken:**
- ✓ 3 oz. chicken breast
- ✓ 1 clove garlic, minced
- ✓ 1 tsp. fresh rosemary, minced
- ✓ 1 tsp. olive oil

**Salad:**
- ✓ 1½ cups greens of choice
- ✓ ½ cup red onion, ½" slices
- ✓ 1 fresh peach, ¼" slices
- ✓ 2 tsp. apple cider vinegar
- ✓ 1 clove garlic, minced
- ✓ Salt and pepper to taste
- ✓ 1 tsp. olive oil
- ✓ Liquid Stevia, to taste (optional)

1. Combine the chicken breast with the marinade ingredients and marinate in the refrigerator for overnight.
2. Preheat the grill to high, about 400°. Place the marinated chicken and onion slices on the grill, and immediately lower the heat to medium.
3. Grill the chicken for 6-8 minutes per side, depending on the thickness. Grill the onions for about 4 minutes per side, or until they have browned grill marks and are starting to soften. Remove chicken and onions and let rest.
4. Layer salad greens, peaches, then warm sliced chicken and onions.
5. Whisk together vinegar, garlic, salt, pepper, and oil, and pour over the salad.

☒ 3 oz of protein

☒ 1 serving of fruit

☒ 2 servings of vegetables

☒ 1-2 servings of healthy fat

# Red Cabbage Citrus Salad

**Salad:**
- ✓ 2 cups cabbage, shredded
- ✓ 1 orange, peeled and sliced
- ✓ ⅛ avocado, diced

**Dressing:**
- ✓ 2 Tbsp. apple cider vinegar
- ✓ 3 Tbsp. lime juice
- ✓ 1 tsp. olive oil
- ✓ ¼ cup cilantro, chopped
- ✓ ½ tsp. chili powder
- ✓ ½ tsp. garlic powder
- ✓ ½ tsp. black pepper
- ✓ ½ tsp. salt

---

1. Put the cabbage in a bowl and set aside.
2. Combine all the dressing ingredients in a jar with a lid and shake until thoroughly mixed.
3. Pour half of the dressing on the cabbage and toss until combined.
4. Top with orange slices and avocado and add more dressing if desired.

☐ 3 oz of protein      ☒ 1 serving of fruit

☒ 2 servings of vegetables      ☒ 1-2 servings of healthy fat

# Lime Chicken Chopped Salad

- ✓ 3 oz. chicken breast
- ✓ 1 Tbsp. paprika
- ✓ Juice of 1 lime
- ✓ ¼ tsp. salt
- ✓ ¼ tsp. black pepper

**Salad:**
- ✓ 1½ cup spring mix
- ✓ 1 peach, sliced
- ✓ ¼ cup grape tomatoes, quartered
- ✓ ¼ cup red onion, finely chopped
- ✓ ⅛ avocado, cubed

**Lime Vinaigrette:**
- ✓ 1 tsp. olive oil
- ✓ 2 Tbsp. apple cider vinegar
- ✓ Juice of 1 lime
- ✓ Dash salt

---

1. Season chicken with salt and pepper. In a bowl, combine paprika and lime juice.
2. Add chicken and let marinate in the refrigerator for at 30 minutes to overnight.
3. Heat the grill to medium and grease lightly.
4. Grill chicken until done and let rest.
5. Cut peach into slices and add to grill for 3-4 minutes on each side.
6. In a serving bowl, add avocado, tomato, red onion, and spring mix.
7. Whisk together vinaigrette ingredients in a small bowl.
8. Slice chicken, and top the salad with the chicken, peaches, and vinaigrette.

☒ 3 oz of protein  ☒ 1 serving of fruit

☒ 2 servings of vegetables  ☒ 1-2 servings of healthy fat

# Cobb Salad

- ✓ 1½ cups spring mix lettuce, packed
- ✓ 1 hard-boiled egg, sliced
- ✓ ⅛ avocado, cubed
- ✓ ¼ cup tomato, chopped
- ✓ ¼ cup red onion, finely chopped
- ✓ 2 oz. cooked, cubed chicken

**Dressing:**
- ✓ 1 tsp. olive oil
- ✓ 1 Tbsp. apple cider vinegar
- ✓ Juice of half a lemon

---

If you are particular about your presentation, place the salad in a bowl and then add the toppings on in rows as the picture. If not, simply place all ingredients in a large mixing bowl, add the dressing, and toss.

☒ 3 oz of protein        ☐ 1 serving of fruit

☒ 2 servings of vegetables    ☒ 1-2 servings of healthy fat

# Steak Cobb Salad with Cilantro Vinaigrette

- ✓ 1 cup romaine lettuce, chopped
- ✓ ½ cup cherry tomatoes, diced
- ✓ 1 hard-boiled egg, sliced
- ✓ ½ cup red onion, sliced
- ✓ ¼ cup pickled jalapeños, sliced
- ✓ 2 oz. steak
- ✓ 1 tsp. coconut oil

**Cilantro-Dijon Vinaigrette:**
- ✓ 1 tsp. olive oil
- ✓ 2 tsp. apple cider vinegar
- ✓ 1 tsp. Dijon mustard
- ✓ Pinch of salt and pepper
- ✓ ¼ cup cilantro, chopped
- ✓ 1 tsp. lemon juice
- ✓ Liquid Stevia to taste(optional)

---

1. Pat the steak dry and season generously with salt and pepper.
2. Heat oil in an oven-safe skillet over high heat. Add the steak and sear on each side for 2 minutes. Turn oven to broil and let steak cook for to desired doneness.
3. Add vinaigrette ingredients into a blender and blend until smooth.
4. To assemble, layer lettuce, tomatoes, egg, red onion, and jalapeños in a salad bowl. Top with sliced steak and vinaigrette.

☒ 3 oz of protein ☐ 1 serving of fruit

☒ 2 servings of vegetables ☒ 1-2 servings of healthy fat

# Spiced Grapefruit and Chicken Watercress Salad

- 3 oz. cooked chicken breast, shredded
- ½ pink grapefruit, segmented, and its juice
- 1 dried red chili
- 1 Tbsp. olive oil
- Salt to taste
- 1 Tbsp. lemon juice
- 1 Tbsp. sumac
- ¼ cup red onion, thinly sliced
- 1½ cups watercress
- ⅓ cup fresh basil leaves roughly chopped
- ¼ cup shallots, chopped

---

1. Cut the grapefruit segments away from each membrane, capturing any juice as you go. Put segments in a bowl and set aside.
2. Pour the juice into a saucepan. Squeeze the other half of the grapefruit if more is needed. Add red chili, bring to a boil, lower heat to medium and simmer until reduced.
3. Set aside to cool, then whisk in the olive oil, lemon juice, salt, and sumac.
4. Cut the watercress from the stems and add to a bowl along with the basil.
5. Gently toss the salad greens with the grapefruit, red onion, chicken, and dressing. Top with shallots and serve.

☒ 3 oz of protein  ☒ 1 serving of fruit

☒ 2 servings of vegetables  ☒ 1-2 servings of healthy fat

# Kale Ginger Detox Salad

- ✓ 1 cup kale
- ✓ ⅓ cup broccoli florets
- ✓ ⅓ cup Brussels sprouts, roughly chopped
- ✓ ⅓ cup red cabbage, roughly chopped
- ✓ ½ cup fresh parsley
- ✓ 6 almonds *or* 1 Tbsp. sunflower seeds

**Dressing:**

- ✓ 1 tsp. olive oil
- ✓ 3 Tbsp. lemon juice
- ✓ 2 tsp. fresh ginger, peeled and grated
- ✓ 1 tsp. Dijon mustard
- ✓ Salt to taste

---

1. Using a food processor, process the first 5 ingredients and mix in a large bowl. This may take a few batches.
2. Add the almonds or sunflower seeds to the food processor, pulse until roughly chopped and mix in with the salad.
3. In a small bowl, whisk together dressing ingredients and drizzle over the salad.

☐ 3 oz of protein              ☐ 1 serving of fruit

☒ 2 servings of vegetables     ☒ 1-2 servings of healthy fat

# Indoor Holiday Celebrations

Holidays are a time for family, friends, and connection to food through celebration. Feeding your body healthful foods allows you to truly connect to the festivities with more energy and life.

"Celebrate the happiness that friends are always giving, make every day a holiday and celebrate just living."

Amanda Bradley

# Healthy Roast Turkey

- ✓ 1 turkey
- ✓ ½ lb. butter
- ✓ ½ tsp. sage
- ✓ ½ tsp. thyme
- ✓ ½ tsp. marjoram
- ✓ ½ tsp. rosemary

---

1. Preheat oven to 425°.
2. Rinse the turkey inside and out, and then pat dry. Stuff (optional) and truss. Cut a piece of cheesecloth to a length that will cover the turkey and unfold to a single thickness.
3. Melt butter in a small saucepan over medium-low heat and add sage, thyme, marjoram, and rosemary. Place cheesecloth in the pan and completely saturate.
4. Place turkey in oven and reduce heat to 325°. After 15 minutes, drape butter-soaked cheesecloth over the turkey so that it is completely covered. After an hour, baste the turkey every 15 minutes or so to keep the cheesecloth moist. Remove the cheesecloth for the last 30 minutes of cooking time for crisp skin. After removing from oven, allow turkey to rest for at least 20 minutes before carving.
5. 1 serving = 3 oz. turkey

☒ 3 oz of protein    ☐ 1 serving of fruit

☐ 2 servings of vegetables    ☒ 1-2 servings of healthy fat

# Mashed No-Tatoes

- ✓ 1 head cauliflower, roughly chopped
- ✓ 1½ Tbsp. butter
- ✓ 1-2 cloves garlic (optional)
- ✓ Salt and pepper to taste

---

1. Steam cauliflower until very soft.
2. Transfer cauliflower to a food processor or blender with butter, salt, pepper, and garlic.
3. Blend to desired consistency.
4. 1 serving = 1 cup

☐ 3 oz of protein     ☐ 1 serving of fruit

☒ 1-2 servings of vegetables     ☒ 1-2 servings of healthy fat

# Green Bean "Cauli" Casserole

- ✓ 6 cups green beans, trimmed and cut
- ✓ 1 Tbsp. olive oil
- ✓ 24 oz. mushrooms, sliced
- ✓ Salt and pepper to taste
- ✓ 2 cloves garlic, minced
- ✓ 1 cup shallots, peeled, and sliced thinly
- ✓ 2 ½ cups "Mashed No-Tatoes"
- ✓ ½ cup slivered almonds
- ✓ Grapeseed oil

---

1. Preheat oven to 350°.
2. Add green beans to a stockpot of salted, boiling water and cook 3-5 minutes, until tender. Transfer to bowl of ice water. Drain and set aside.
3. Heat oil in large skillet over medium-high heat. Add mushrooms and cook 10-12 minutes, stirring frequently, until dry. Add salt and pepper.
4. Reduce heat to medium-low and add garlic for another 2-3 minutes. Add "Mashed No-Tatoes" and stir to combine. Heat thoroughly, stirring occasionally. Add green beans.
5. Grease a 9"x 13" casserole dish with grapeseed oil. Transfer green bean mixture to dish and top with slivered almonds. Bake 25-30 minutes.
6. Makes 6 servings. 1 serving = 1 cup

- ☐ 3 oz of protein
- ☒ 1-2 servings of vegetables
- ☐ 1 serving of fruit
- ☒ 1-2 servings of healthy fat

# Cauliflower Pizza

- 2 cups cauliflower florets
- ¼ tsp. salt
- ½ tsp. basil
- ½ tsp. oregano
- ½ tsp. garlic powder
- 2 Tbsp. almond meal
- 1 Tbsp. olive oil
- 1 egg, beaten
- Oil for brushing
- Few shakes of crushed red pepper

**Toppings:**
- 6 oz. cooked chicken, shredded
- ½ cup sautéed mushrooms
- ⅛ avocado
- ½ cup tomato sauce
- Fresh basil

1. Preheat oven to 450°. Line a cutting board with a large piece of parchment paper and brush with oil.
2. Pulse cauliflower florets in a food processor for about 30 seconds, until powdery and snow-like.
3. Measure out 2 cups and transfer to a microwave-safe bowl. Cover and microwave for 4 minutes.
4. Turn out the cauliflower onto a clean tea towel. When cauliflower is cool enough to handle, wrap it up in the dish towel and wring, squeezing out as much water as possible.
5. Transfer cauliflower back to the bowl and add spices, almond meal, and oil. Mix with your hands to incorporate all the ingredients, then add egg and mix again. Press the dough into a crust on the parchment paper.

6. Using a cutting board, slide the parchment paper onto the hot pizza stone or baking sheet in the oven. Bake for about 12 minutes, or until it starts to turn golden brown.
7. Remove from oven and add toppings. Slide pizza back in the oven and bake for another 5 minutes.
8. Makes 2 servings. 1 serving = half pizza

- ☒ 3 oz of protein
- ☐ 1 serving of fruit
- ☒ 2 servings of vegetables
- ☒ 1-2 servings of healthy fat

# Healthful Chili

- ✓ 1½ lbs. ground beef
- ✓ 2 cloves garlic, minced
- ✓ 3 Tbsp. olive oil
- ✓ 1½ cups onion, diced
- ✓ ½ cup celery, chopped
- ✓ 2 Tbsp. chili powder
- ✓ 1 tsp. cumin
- ✓ 1 tsp. oregano
- ✓ 1 tsp. salt
- ✓ ¼ tsp. cayenne pepper
- ✓ 4 cups zucchini, diced
- ✓ 14-oz. can tomato sauce
- ✓ 14-oz. can diced tomatoes

1. In a large pot, thoroughly brown beef, and garlic over medium heat. Drain excess fat and set aside.
2. Heat oil in a skillet over medium-high heat. Add onions, celery, and seasonings, and sauté for 5-7 minutes. When onions are golden and veggies are halfway cooked, add zucchini and cook for 2 more minutes, stirring frequently.
3. Add skillet ingredients into the pot and stir well. Also add tomatoes and bring everything to a boil, stirring frequently. Reduce heat and simmer for 20 minutes.
4. Makes 8 servings. 1 serving = approximately 1 cup

☒ 3 oz of protein  ☐ 1 serving of fruit

☒ 1 serving of vegetables  ☒ 1-2 servings of healthy fat

# Delicious Broccoli and Cauliflower Rice

- 1 cup cauliflower florets
- 1 cup broccoli florets
- 2 tsp. olive oil
- 1 tsp. garlic powder
- Salt and pepper to taste

---

1. Preheat oven to 350°.
2. Process cauliflower and broccoli florets in a food processor until riced.
3. Transfer the mixture to a large baking sheet in a single layer. Season with salt, pepper, and oil.
4. Bake for 10 minutes. Remove from oven and stir and bake for another 10 minutes. Repeat until golden.
5. Makes 1 serving.

- ☐ 3 oz of protein
- ☒ 2 servings of vegetables
- ☐ 1 serving of fruit
- ☒ 1-2 servings of healthy fat

# Mock Sweet Potato Casserole

- ✓ 4 cups cauliflower florets
- ✓ 1 cup cooked pumpkin
- ✓ ¾ tsp. liquid Stevia
- ✓ 3 eggs
- ✓ ½ tsp. salt

- ✓ 2 Tbsp. butter, softened
- ✓ 1 tsp. cinnamon
- ✓ 1 tsp. nutmeg
- ✓ ½ tsp. ginger

---

1. Preheat oven to 325°. Steam cauliflower until soft.
2. Add cauliflower, pumpkin, and ginger in food processor or blender. Purée until smooth.
3. Spread mixture into a 2 quart or 11"x 17" dish and bake for 30 minutes.
4. Makes 3 servings. 1 serving = approximately 1 cup

☐ 3 oz of protein

☐ 1 serving of fruit

☒ 1-2 servings of vegetables

☒ 1-2 servings of healthy fat

# Baked Apple

- ✓ 2 tsp. butter, divided
- ✓ 1 green apple, no more than ⅛" slices
- ✓ ¼ tsp. cinnamon

---

1. Preheat oven to 350°.
2. Melt 1 tsp. butter in an oven-safe skillet.
3. Start layering the apple slices into the dish, slightly overlapping them. Work from the outside to the inside.
4. Sprinkle cinnamon on top of the apples and dot the extra tsp. of butter over the top.
5. Bake for about 20 minutes or until the apple has softened and begun to brown slightly at the edges.

☐ 3 oz of protein         ☒ 1 serving of fruit

☐ 2 servings of vegetables    ☒ 1-2 servings of healthy fat

# Cranberry Sauce

- ✓ 12 oz. fresh or frozen cranberries
- ✓ 1 cup xylitol
- ✓ 1 cup water
- ✓ ½ tsp. cinnamon
- ✓ Grated orange zest to taste

---

1. Bring water and xylitol to a boil in a medium saucepan.
2. Add cranberries to water and return to a boil.
3. Add cinnamon and orange zest.
4. Reduce heat and boil gently for 10 minutes, stirring occasionally.
5. Pour sauce into serving bowl. Cover and cool completely at room temperature or refrigerate.
6. Serving size = ½ cup

☐ 3 oz of protein   ☒ 1 serving of fruit

☐ 2 servings of vegetables   ☐ 1-2 servings of healthy fat

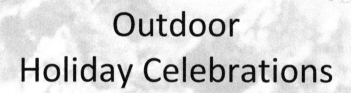

# Outdoor Holiday Celebrations

Barbeques and other outdoor celebrations are a time to kick back, relax, and enjoy the beauty of nature. You can still feed your body healthfully with these amazing recipes and enjoy all that the outdoor seasons offer in celebration!

"The more you praise and celebrate your life, the more there is in life to be celebrated."

Oprah Winfrey

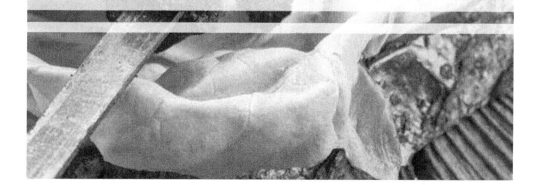

# Sweet and Crunchy Chicken Slaw

- 1 cup red cabbage, shredded
- ⅔ cup white cabbage, shredded
- ⅓ cup scallions, chopped
- 3 oz. cooked chicken, shredded
- 6 slivered almonds
- 1 tsp. butter
- 1 Tbsp. pumpkin seeds
- 1 Tbsp. apple cider vinegar
- 1 tsp. olive oil
- 1 Tbsp. Bragg's Liquid Aminos
- Liquid Stevia (optional)

---

1. In a bowl, mix red cabbage, white cabbage, and chicken.
2. In a small bowl, whisk together apple cider vinegar, oil, Bragg's Liquid Aminos, and Stevia.
3. Add dressing to the cabbage and chicken and mix well.
4. Heat butter in a pan and sauté almonds and pumpkin seeds for 2-4 minutes.
5. Add almonds, pumpkin seeds, and scallions to the cabbage and chicken and mix well.

☒ 3 oz of protein  
☐ 1 serving of fruit  
☒ 2 servings of vegetables  
☒ 1-2 servings of healthy fat

# Easy Veggie Salad

- ½ cup cucumbers, finely chopped
- ½ cup tomatoes, finely chopped
- ¼ cup red onion, finely chopped
- ¼ cup green pepper, finely chopped
- ½ cup cauliflower, riced
- ⅓ cup fresh Italian parsley, finely chopped
- 1-2 tsp. olive oil
- 1 Tbsp. lemon juice
- Salt and pepper to taste
- Garlic to taste (optional)
- ⅓ cup scallions, finely chopped (optional)

---

1. Combine cucumbers, tomatoes, onion, and parsley in a large mixing bowl.
2. Pour oil and lemon juice over vegetables and mix well to coat. Add scallions, garlic, salt, pepper, and cauliflower rice, and mix well to combine.
3. Cover and refrigerate until ready to serve.

☐ 3 oz of protein   ☐ 1 serving of fruit

☒ 2 servings of vegetables   ☒ 1-2 servings of healthy fat

# Baked Cinnamon Apple Chips

- ✓ 1 Granny Smith apple, ⅛" slices
- ✓ 1 tsp. cinnamon

---

1. Preheat oven to 200°.  Line a baking sheet with parchment paper
2. Arrange apple slices on baking sheet in a single layer.  Sprinkle cinnamon over apples.
3. Bake for approximately 1 hour, then turn.  Continue baking for 1-2 hours, turning occasionally, until the apple slices are no longer moist.  Store in airtight container.

☐ 3 oz of protein                    ☒ 1 serving of fruit

☐ 2 servings of vegetables    ☐ 1-2 servings of healthy fat

# Chicken Wings

- ✓ 2 lbs. chicken wings

**Dry Rub:**
- ✓ 1 Tbsp. garlic powder
- ✓ 1 Tbsp. cayenne pepper
- ✓ 1 Tbsp. dry mustard
- ✓ 1 Tbsp. black pepper
- ✓ 2 tsp. cumin

**Sauce:**
- ✓ 4 Tbsp. butter
- ✓ 2 Tbsp. olive oil
- ✓ 2 Tbsp. reserved dry rub
- ✓ 12-oz. Frank's hot sauce
- ✓ 1 Tbsp. apple cider vinegar

1. Combine all dry rub spices in a large bowl. Reserve 2 Tbsp. of the mixture.
2. Add wings to the bowl and coat thoroughly. Cover and refrigerate for at least an hour.
3. Preheat oven to 375° and line a baking sheet with parchment paper.
4. Lay wings flat on the baking sheet and bake for an hour, turning halfway through.
5. When the wings are almost done, melt the butter in a saucepan and add other sauce ingredients.
6. When ready to serve, add the wings to a large serving bowl, pour sauce over the wings and toss.
7. Each wing has approximately ½ oz. protein. 6 wings = 1 serving

☒ 3 oz of protein  ☐ 1 serving of fruit

☐ 2 servings of vegetables  ☒ 1-2 servings of healthy fat

# Turkey Sliders and Avocado Slaw

**For the Burgers:**
- ✓ 1 lb. ground turkey
- ✓ ¼ red onion, minced
- ✓ ½ poblano pepper, diced
- ✓ ½ red bell pepper, diced
- ✓ 1 tsp. cumin
- ✓ Salt and pepper to taste
- ✓ 1 Tbsp. olive oil

**For the Slaw:**
- ✓ 1 small head cabbage, chopped (or bag of cabbage)
- ✓ 2 avocados
- ✓ 1 Tbsp. olive oil
- ✓ 1 tsp. lime juice
- ✓ ½ tsp. lemon juice
- ✓ 1 tsp. cumin
- ✓ ½ tsp. crushed red pepper
- ✓ Salt and pepper to taste

1. Mix all burger ingredients in a large bowl. Shape into 5 patties.
2. Heat a large skillet over medium heat with a bit of oil and add your sliders. Flip after about 3-5 minutes or when you see the sides begin to turn a white color.
3. Put cabbage in a large bowl. Add all other slaw ingredients to a food processor and pulse until smooth.
4. Add to the cabbage and mix. Top off with a bit of salt and pepper.
5. Makes 5 servings. 1 serving = 3 oz. turkey burger and 1-2 cups avocado slaw.

- ☒ 3 oz of protein
- ☐ 1 serving of fruit
- ☒ 2 servings of vegetables
- ☒ 1-2 servings of healthy fat

# Spaghetti and Meatball Bites

- ✓ 1 medium spaghetti squash, cut in half lengthwise, seeds removed
- ✓ 1 lb. ground beef
- ✓ 14-oz. can tomato sauce
- ✓ 3 egg whites, beaten
- ✓ 1 Tbsp. parsley
- ✓ 1 Tbsp. basil
- ✓ 1 Tbsp. thyme
- ✓ Salt and pepper to taste
- ✓ 1 Tbsp. olive oil

1. Preheat oven to 425° and lightly grease a baking sheet.
2. Place spaghetti squash open side down on the baking sheet and bake for 20-25 minutes.
3. In a large bowl, combine ground beef, parsley, basil, thyme, salt, and pepper. Form into 12 bite-sized meatballs.
4. Heat oil in a large skillet over medium heat, then add the meatballs and brown for 3-4 minutes, flipping once.
5. Add tomato sauce and let simmer. Add extra seasonings as desired.
6. Remove squash from oven and use a fork to thread the squash. Turn oven down to 350°. Place silicone cups in a muffin tin and add squash threads to each cup, making a well in the middle of each cup for the meatball to sit.
7. When the meatballs are done cooking, remove them from the sauce and place each in a cup. Pour a bit of egg white on top of each cup.
8. Bake for 18-20 minutes or until egg is completely cooked through.
9. 1 serving = 2 "muffins"

- ☒ 3 oz of protein
- ☐ 1 serving of fruit
- ☒ 2 servings of vegetables
- ☒ 1-2 servings of healthy fat

# Jalapeño Deviled Eggs

- ✓ 6 eggs
- ✓ ¼ cup Vegenaise
- ✓ 1 Tbsp. minced jalapeño (reserve some for garnish)
- ✓ ⅛ tsp. smoked paprika
- ✓ ¼ tsp. salt

---

1. Bring a large pot of water to boil. Add eggs to boiling water and cook for 15 minutes. Remove from water and place in a bowl of cold water.
2. After eggs have cooled, peel and cut eggs in half. Scoop out the yolks, place yolks in a bowl and smash with a fork. Add Vegenaise and mix until smooth.
3. Add jalapeño, paprika, and salt and mix well.
4. Place the mixture into a small Ziploc bag, cut off the end and squeeze mixture into egg white halves. Garnish with reserved jalapeño. Chill before serving.
5. 1 serving = 4 egg halves

☒ 3 oz of protein           ☐ 1 serving of fruit

☐ 2 servings of vegetables  ☒ 1-2 servings of healthy fat

# Salmon Dip

- ✓ 3-4 oz. salmon fillet
- ✓ Pinch of salt
- ✓ Grapeseed oil spray
- ✓ Balsamic vinegar
- ✓ 1 Tbsp. grapeseed oil
- ✓ Mrs. Dash (any variety)
- ✓ 1 Tbsp. Vegenaise

---

1. Preheat oven to 350°.
2. Spray or grease 9"x 11" dish.  Place fillet in dish and pour balsamic oil liberally over fillet.  Pour 1 Tbsp. grapeseed oil over fish.
3. Liberally season with Mrs. Dash and a pinch of salt.  Bake for 30 minutes until fish flakes easily.
4. Let cool 5 to 10 minutes.  Place fish in a bowl and flake with a fork.
5. Add 1 Tbsp. Vegenaise and mix until consistency of dip.

☒ 3 oz of protein  ☐ 1 serving of fruit

☐ 2 servings of vegetables  ☒ 1-2 servings of healthy fat

# Low-Carb Cauliflower Hummus

- ✓ 4 cups cauliflower florets
- ✓ 2 Tbsp. water
- ✓ 5 Tbsp. olive oil, divided
- ✓ 1 tsp. salt, divided
- ✓ 2½ tsp. garlic, minced, divided
- ✓ 1½ Tbsp. tahini paste
- ✓ 3 Tbsp. lemon juice
- ✓ Paprika (optional)

1. Combine cauliflower, water, 2 Tbsp. oil, ½ tsp. salt, and 1½ tsp. garlic in a microwave-safe dish. Microwave uncovered for about 15 minutes or until softened and darkened in color.
2. Put mixture in a blender or food processor. Add the tahini paste, lemon juice, 1 tsp. minced garlic, 3 Tbsp. olive oil and ½ tsp. salt, and blend until smooth.
3. To serve, place the hummus in a bowl and drizzle with extra olive oil and a sprinkle of paprika.
4. Makes 2 servings. 1 serving = 1 cup

☐ 3 oz of protein  ☐ 1 serving of fruit

☒ 1-2 servings of vegetables  ☒ 1-2 servings of healthy fat

# Mock-Tails

### Poolside Bubble
- ✓ 12 oz. chilled seltzer water
- ✓ ½ orange, sliced
- ✓ ½ lime, sliced
- ✓ 2 drops liquid Stevia

Combine all ingredients and serve over ice.

### Fruity Hibiscus Refresher
- ✓ 8 oz. chilled hibiscus tea
- ✓ ½ orange, sliced and squeezed
- ✓ 4 drops liquid Stevia
- ✓ 1 lemon slice
- ✓ 1 lime slice

Combine all ingredients and serve over ice.

# Mock-Tails

### Orange Ginger Spritzer
- 8 oz. chilled seltzer water
- 1 tsp. grated ginger
- ½ orange, juiced
- 1 orange slice
- 4 drops liquid Stevia

Combine all ingredients and serve over ice.

### Orange-Lemonade Mock Tail
- 8 oz. chilled seltzer water
- Juice of half a lemon
- Juice of half an orange
- 5 drops liquid Stevia

Combine all ingredients and serve over ice

### Lime Turmeric Tonic
- 8 oz. chilled seltzer water
- ¼ tsp. turmeric
- Juice of half a lime
- 1 slice lime
- 4 drops liquid Stevia

Combine all ingredients and serve over ice.

# Desserts

Desserts can be a delicious and nutritious way to end a meal. These healthful recipes are a great way to create the beginning of a beautiful, energized evening.

"Work is the meat of life,
pleasure the dessert."
B. C. Forbes

# Grilled Peaches

- ✓ 1 ripe peach
- ✓ ¼ cup almonds, chopped
- ✓ 1-2 tsp. cinnamon
- ✓ 1 tsp. melted coconut oil
- ✓ Liquid Stevia to taste (optional)

---

1. Slice the peach in half and place face up on plate. Drizzle with coconut oil and season generously with cinnamon.
2. Transfer face-down to hot grill and let cook for 8-12 minutes.
3. Remove and top with almonds and liquid Stevia.

☐ 3 oz of protein   ☒ 1 serving of fruit

☐ 2 servings of vegetables   ☒ 1-2 servings of healthy fat

# Adam's Applesauce

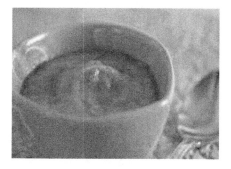

- ✓ 3 lbs. green apples, cored and sliced
- ✓ 12 oz. frozen raspberries or strawberries
- ✓ 1 tsp. cinnamon
- ✓ ⅓ cup water

---

1. Combine ingredients in crockpot and cook on low for 4 hours. Remove lid and cook 30 more minutes.
2. Mash using a potato masher.
3. Sweeten to taste with Stevia.
4. 1 serving = 4 oz.

☐ 3 oz of protein         ☒ 1 serving of fruit

☐ 2 servings of vegetables    ☐ 1-2 servings of healthy fat

# Sweet Blackberry Compote

- ✓ 1 cup frozen blackberries
- ✓ 2 Tbsp. water
- ✓ 10 drops liquid Stevia
- ✓ 1 tsp. vanilla extract

---

1. Put all ingredients into saucepan.
2. Let lightly simmer for 10 minutes until fruit has softened and broken open.
3. Serve alone or on top of pancakes.

☐ 3 oz of protein  ☒ 1 serving of fruit

☐ 2 servings of vegetables  ☐ 1-2 servings of healthy fat

# Charlie's Apple Crumble

**Filling:**
- 9 Granny Smith apples, peeled and chopped
- Juice of 1 lemon
- Zest of 1 lemon
- ½ cup water
- 40 drops liquid Stevia
- 1½ tsp cinnamon
- Pinch of ginger
- Pinch of allspice
- Pinch of nutmeg

**For the topping:**
- 1 cup almond flour *or* ¾ cup almond flour and ¼ almond slivers
- 1 Tbsp. melted butter

---

1. Preheat oven to 350°.
2. Heat all filling ingredients in a saucepan over medium heat and cook for 5-7 minutes, stirring frequently, until apples soften slightly.
3. Combine almond flour and 1 Tbsp. melted butter in bowl.
4. In an 8"x 8" baking dish, add apple mixture. Sprinkle almond flour and butter mixture over top of apples and sprinkle slivered almonds sparingly over top.
5. Bake for 20 minutes.
6. Makes 9 servings.

☐ 3 oz of protein  ☒ 1 serving of fruit

☐ 2 servings of vegetables  ☒ 1-2 servings of healthy fat

# Kaiya's Balsamic Peach Compote

- ✓ 1 cup diced peaches, frozen or fresh
- ✓ 1 tsp. balsamic vinegar
- ✓ 2 Tbsp. water
- ✓ Liquid Stevia to taste

---

1. Heat peaches, water, and liquid Stevia in a saucepan.
2. Let simmer for 10 minutes until peaches have softened.
3. Add balsamic vinegar and let simmer for 5 more minutes.
4. Cool slightly and serve alone or on top of pancakes

☐ 3 oz of protein ☒ 1 serving of fruit

☐ 2 servings of vegetables ☐ 1-2 servings of healthy fat

# About the Authors

# Dr. Kristen Kells, DC, BSC

Dr. Kristen Kells owns several large natural health-care clinics within the USA. With over 20 years of experience in private practice, she has helped thousands of patients reach their health and wellness goals. As an expert in her field, Dr. Kells has been asked to speak in a variety of settings from small groups, church events, corporate wellness programs, to lecturing nationally and internationally to other health-care professionals.

In addition, Dr. Kells has had the immense honor of working with Team USA Wrestling and Judo athletes to help them reach their peak performance. As a part of their support team, Dr. Kells attended the games in London 2012 and in Rio 2016 as Team Chiropractor. In 2008, Dr. Kells was awarded Woman of the Year by USA Wrestling for her commitment and servitude.

At the age of 33, Dr. Kristen Kells weighed over 200 lbs. and was stressed out, burned out, and starting to feel hopeless. Like many of her clients, she was frustrated with the yo-yo diets, incomplete programs, and confusing, contradictory advice that left her worse off than when she started. She realized that not only did something have to change for her and her family, but the way we approach weight loss in America had to be reinvented. That realization began her journey to build a program with incredible weight loss results and long-term health transformation.
After losing 80 pounds and keeping it off for over 15 years, Dr. Kells pulled together her research, clinical experience, and personal health journey to build a program that works! Dr. Kells' Weight Loss Program is clinically proven, science-backed, and results in long-term weight loss and health transformation.

# Wendi Francis MS, RD, CPC

Wendi Francis MS, RD, CPC is a pioneer in her field with specialty areas in food psychology and eating issues.

She is a graduate-level registered dietitian with extensive certifications in multiple areas of psychology and nutrition. Wendi has worked in her own private practice and business for over 25 years, facilitating permanent transformation for others by turning their fears around food into freedom.

She is a best-selling author, facilitative entrepreneur, podcast personality, recognized speaker, and educator.

In this recipe book, Wendi brings the inspiration to make creative cooking changes to your food, enabling you to live the healthful life you were designed to live

Made in the USA
Middletown, DE
12 July 2022

69060378R00096